MW00818117

# Coming Home to Passion

# COMING HOME TO PASSION

### Restoring Loving Sexuality in Couples with Histories of Childhood Trauma and Neglect

Ruth Cohn

Sex, Love, and Psychology
*Judy Kuriansky, Series Editor*

 PRAEGER

AN IMPRINT OF ABC-CLIO, LLC
Santa Barbara, California • Denver, Colorado • Oxford, England

**Library of Congress Cataloging-in-Publication Data**

Cohn, Ruth, 1955–
  Coming home to passion : restoring loving sexuality in couples with histories of childhood trauma and neglect / Ruth Cohn.
      p. cm. — (Sex, love, and psychology)
  Includes bibliographical references and index.
  ISBN 978-0-313-39212-2 (hard copy : alk. paper) — ISBN 978-0-313-39213-9 (eBook)
1. Couples therapy. 2. Sex therapy. 3. Psychic trauma in children. 4. Adult child abuse victims.
I. Title.
  [DNLM: 1. Couples Therapy. 2. Marital Therapy. 3. Adult Survivors of Child Abuse—
psychology. 4. Love. 5. Sexuality—psychology. 6. Spouses—psychology. WM 430.5.M3]
RC488.5.C633  2011
616.89′1562—dc22            2010043753

ISBN: 978-0-313-39212-2
EISBN: 978-0-313-39213-9

15  14  13  12  11      1  2  3  4  5

This book is also available on the World Wide Web as an eBook.
Visit www.abc-clio.com for details.

Praeger
An Imprint of ABC-CLIO, LLC

ABC-CLIO, LLC
130 Cremona Drive, P.O. Box 1911
Santa Barbara, California 93116-1911

This book is printed on acid-free paper ∞

Manufactured in the United States of America

To my mom, who died too soon.

And to all those children, born and unborn,
alive because their parents had the mettle
and the heart to do this work.

# CONTENTS

# SERIES FOREWORD

What do popular rock lyrics like those of John Lennon and brain twisters from the Talmud have to do with attachment theorist John Bowlby and relationship therapist Harville Hendrix? Plenty, as author and marriage and family therapist Ruth Cohn cleverly weaves references to cultural icons with solid psychological theory in her book *Coming Home to Passion: Restoring Loving Sexuality in Couples with Histories of Childhood Trauma and Neglect.*

A couples counselor and sex therapist certified by the American Association of Sex Educators, Counselors and Therapists, Cohn explains that Lennon experienced trauma in his life that appears linked to healing in his album *Double Fantasy*. Similarly, Cohn describes the journeys of her patients who have suffered from trauma, including sessions and techniques that helped them heal.

The importance of Cohn's topic is indisputable, with statistics indicating that up to one in four women and one in seven men have been abused in some way. Add to those shocking numbers that many men and women suffer from widespread neglect, pain, or trauma from life experiences and/or past relationships, leading to potent reasons for the large percentage of men and women who suffer resulting sexual problems. For this reason, Cohn's book is an important one—for couples and for professionals alike—as she clearly outlines the theories of trauma and the processes for recovery. Cohn uses her knowledge of Bowlby's attachment theory, Hendrix's Imago therapy, defense mechanisms, behavioral patterns, and even brain circuitry, combined with adaptations of proven sexual therapy techniques and her own creative approaches, to show how people suffering from trauma can emerge into relationship and sexual intimacy. The book's professional foundation is made into accessible—and enjoyable—reading by references like those to Wimbledon as a metaphor for couples' interactions, and to chiaroscuro (as used in art) as a metaphor for processing emotional shadows into light. Many stories stand out, including Cohn's personal one about a partner who disappoints her by not appreciating gifts until his traumatic history is revealed: that his mother bought gifts for him that pleased *her* instead of him. The analogy to a gold standard in sex therapy is clear: please a partner by doing what he or she wants rather than what you desire for yourself.

Cohn's personal and empathic style exudes warmth that draws the reader in. A wide audience can benefit greatly by following the cases she describes and feeling comforted through the processing of pain. And professionals will find the specifics of theory and sessions helpful to apply in their own practice of relationship and sexual therapy. As a professional relationship and sex therapist myself, I resonated with and appreciated her techniques, such as the Life Boat, which outlines steps to emotional repair. And as an author and avid reader, I was impressed with her engaging style. Cohn's hope and optimism cannot help but inspire.

All therapists know the importance of communication for a healthy and intimate relationship. Cohn introduces us to another creative metaphor: "HD communication," which she describes as sharpening our focus. Her book is proof of how such a focus works to overcome a history of trauma and neglect and restore loving sexuality.

Dr. Judy Kuriansky

# ACKNOWLEDGMENTS

My three greatest teachers are men. My Dad, Hans Cohn, came through the Holocaust intrepid, tireless, and intent on making the world a better place. He taught me to face pain and injustice squarely, relentlessly, and with undying faith and optimism, and that with hard work one can surmount most anything. These are all good principles with which to approach relationship.

Bessel van der Kolk, vanguard of the trauma field, has been the beacon of my career for most of thirty years. Over and over he pointed the searchlight on what was to be my next step and exposed me to many of the other thinkers and practitioners who would most shape my work. I cannot thank him enough.

And my husband Michael Lewin, who inspired my foundational conviction that a partner committed to working on relationship through the lifespan makes virtually anything possible; and healing in the partnership is the most profound experience I know of. He is my co-author in life.

My three greatest mentors are women. Joan Cole has enriched my whole life for more than thirty years and taught me attachment theory long before I had any idea what that was.

Sallie Foley, almost from the first moment we met, extended warm, fresh, and astonishing encouragement that lit a fire under me to find a publisher.

And Pat Love, whose work I followed and admired for years before I got to know her personally. When I did, she was even more brilliant, kind, and authentic than the idealized image I had conjured. She taught me also the meaning of mentoring and how I might strive to pass it on. All three of these women have stood as the role models I had always craved and sought.

I am blessed with family: two wonderful sisters, Becki Cohn Vargas and Barbara Liepman, who, along with their families, supported and proudly cheered me along, and who patiently forgave my unavailability. My dear friends believed in me and kept in touch when time seemed ever to sneak away from me, most especially Laura Lubin and Dawn Hawk, who painstakingly and lovingly read and edited every chapter.

The early-morning crowd at World Gym unwittingly constituted a comforting, blurry backdrop as inspiration, respiration, and perspiration conspired to gestate some of my best prose. And last but hardly least, I am infinitely grateful to my courageous clients over the decades, who entrusted me with the privilege of sharing in their sacred journeys. May love and passion ever fill your homes. Thank you all!

# INTRODUCTION

The inspiration that spawned this work began now more than two decades ago. It was a confluence of several powerful forces. I began my career as a psychotherapist specializing in trauma. Many of my clients were women who had been sexually abused in childhood. Many of them had partners, and in therapy I heard a frequent refrain: "My partner does not understand!" "My partner resents the therapy bills." "My partner hounds me for sex." "I am so lonely in this relationship . . ." Trauma therapy, at least for a time, is the centerpiece of one's life. It troubled me that in the course of that long sojourn, my client might grow to feel closer to me than to her partner or spouse. It occurred to me that I needed to work with these partners, to teach them about trauma so they would be better support for my clients. I set out to offer workshops for partners of survivors of childhood sexual abuse.

When I offered the first such workshop I had a humbling surprise. That group of men (and the first group was all male) had much to teach me. I encountered a diverse gathering: a prolific author, a doctor, an electrician, a theologian, the CFO of a Fortune 500 company, a schoolteacher. Their ages ranged from 30 to 72. They were of a variety of races and religions. What they had in common, besides being "sex-starved," was that all of them had histories of childhood neglect. Of course I did not discern this immediately. It took time to come into focus. Invariably as each partner introduced himself to the group, each told the dramatic, painful story of his partner or spouse. It was as if they did not have stories of their own. In fact, many of them did not realize that they themselves had stories.

Perhaps what is most insidious about neglect is that it can be so invisible. This can confound both child and adult. They can truthfully say "nothing happened to *me*." Precisely! *Nothing* happened. A host of essential experiences that are supposed to happen are silently missing. I began to see that somehow, these adult children of neglect seemed to pair up with adult children of trauma. Together they created a painful and remarkably homogenous constellation of relationship dynamics.

The men were astonished and relieved to learn how much they had in common with each other. Already I had to revise my ideas. My carefully crafted workshop designed to teach them about trauma and the brain and how to be better partners to my clients transformed itself into a journey of discovery for the partners themselves. Meanwhile, my discovery was that these couples, composed of a survivor of trauma and a survivor of neglect, were somehow recreating their childhoods together, and *both* needed to learn how to be better support to the other.

I have never been able to make my peace with how long therapy, and trauma therapy in particular, takes. It strikes me as grossly unjust that after suffering a violent, humiliating, lonely or otherwise painful childhood, the adult might spend years of time and large sums of money just to be able to live with tranquility in the present. It also disturbed me that the therapy arrangement was such that it ends in loss: that a client would invest years, engaging in a profoundly intimate alliance with the therapist in which to heal, perhaps having a first experience of trust and safety with another person, and when the healing reaches its successful completion, by design the relationship ends. It seemed an ironic booby prize: reaching one's goal means losing the person. In body building the cliché is "failure is success." In this case, gain is loss. I wondered what it would be like if my traumatized clients could discover their safety, trust, and healing in relationships that they would then get to take home and keep. It made a lot of sense to me. Imago Relationship Therapy offered a model that compelled and deeply influenced me. Its echoes reverberate through this book.

I must add that as with many of my greatest mentors and role models, my most convincing research laboratory has been my own life. Journeying from the bleak, energy-leaching despair of chronic disconnection and conflict to a state of sweet and peaceful partnership in my own marriage was perhaps the most profound experience of my life. It was probably also the most difficult. But having traveled that rocky road myself sustains my undying faith that this healing journey is both possible and worth it.

To be sure, there are couples for whom sex is not a problem or not important. They may benefit from the relationship-repairing aspect of this book. My work, however, has brought me an overwhelming proportion of couples for whom the interplay of their trauma and neglect histories has created devastating sexual difficulties and often longstanding sexual impasses. Mired in their often enduring, persistent, and demoralizing dynamics, they have struggled to sustain any hope at all that change might be possible, let alone know how to begin. For many of the traumatized, particularly the sexually traumatized, sex is a final healing frontier. Because the antithesis of trauma is safety, and because safety is the solid foundation upon which loving and lively sexuality rests, restoring safety in the sexual body is a pinnacle of trauma recovery. Making that journey in the company of one's partner is in itself a previously unknown experience of relationship safety. It is my hope that this book will serve as a map.

The book is organized in four parts. Part I is a primer about relationship. It works up from the basics because I take as given that the more difficult and painful one's childhood, the more difficult, painful, and challenging one's adult relationships will be. This is not a point of shame. It is certainly not your fault that relationship might be an area of agony in what might otherwise seem a fairly successful life. Rather, this fact is another of the gross injustices, perhaps even the gravest of all, that comes with trauma and neglect. Part I details this, beginning in Chapter 1 with an explanation of how some fundamental relationship patterns begin. Understanding the origins of styles and patterns of relating can help partners to take each other's upsetting behaviors less personally, perhaps introducing compassion instead, even while working to change those behaviors.

Chapter 2 introduces the complex concepts of differentness, empathy, and boundary. It can be a jarring revelation to discover how different one's partner is from oneself and that some of the essential features of one's worldview are not universal. We need not be the same to be compatible or connected. We can be unique and separate and still very close as long as we feel free to be ourselves and as long as we both feel understood.

Chapter 3 is a practical guide to communication. It is almost cliché how crucial communication is to relationship. This chapter offers concrete tools and guideposts for both speaking and listening, "arts" that are both utterly simple and yet steeply difficult.

Chapter 4 speaks to the requisite need to tip the balance of positive to negative interaction in order for the relationship to stabilize and thrive. Individuals with painful histories, depression, or both are inclined to both communicate and interpret their partners' communication with a negative spin. This chapter shines a light on these dynamics and proposes approaches to improving the positive climate.

Chapter 5 cites anthropology, physiology, and history in naming some possibly generic and hard-wired differences between the genders. When normalized and better understood, such differences might appear less like untenable obstacles or personal insults.

Part II is a brief introductory course on trauma and neglect. Chapter 6 focuses on trauma, with a particular interest in its impact on the nervous system. I am endlessly fascinated with the infinite complexity of the human brain, and I have repeatedly seen how compassion is enhanced and blame diminished, for both self and partner, through understanding physiology and its impact on behavior. Dynamics that make a minefield of daily life can be both comprehended and transformed.

Chapter 7 shines its spotlight on the widely neglected, devastating experience of neglect. Although there is far less research on neglect, it is rapidly becoming clear that it can be equally or even more injurious than the more overt forms of traumatic experience. Personally, I view neglect as a category of trauma. One of my frustrations with the literature to date has been that traditionally the more overtly traumatized partner has garnered "all the blame and all the help." The child of neglect somehow has continued to be neglected. This book seeks to level the playing field for the benefit of both. For the adult survivor of neglect, discovering "I have a story too" can be an enlightening and exciting homecoming. For the trauma survivor, this can be a great relief: "You mean it's not all my fault?"

Chapter 8 examines the fundamental concept of "triggering," examining both its behavioral and physiological aspects. Partners restimulate each other's deepest historical vulnerabilities and hurts, activating the age-old reactions utilized to adapt to those hurts. The result is an agonizing, draining, and exhaustingly redundant patterned interaction in which together the couple unwittingly and unintentionally re-enacts the worst childhood experiences of both. Awareness of the patterns is key to beginning the work of stopping this reckless train.

Chapter 9 continues the conversation about triggering, illustrating how an initially seemingly minor or innocent misstep can culminate in a disproportionately huge rupture between partners due to a ricochet of reactivity. It traces how this happens and describes the work of how to disarm the dynamic. It also drives home the essential point that it invariably takes two to escalate, which is another good reason to gain mastery over one's own triggering tendencies.

Chapter 10 discusses the immeasurable value of repair. For most survivors of trauma and neglect, relationship repair is an unknown experience. Most, after they were hurt, were routinely left alone to reconstitute themselves from the episode and to figure out any possible way to restore the lost connection. Repair requires effort and skill and is of course a requisite for relationship. There will always be some measure of conflict and ebbing of connection in even the most successful relationship. Knowing how to restore connection makes relationship infinitely safer and easier. The chapter also offers a potent repair tool for use in some of the most problematic or entrenched ruptures.

Part III is the fundamental sex education that most of us never had. Chapter 11 introduces the topic and emphasizes how open and frank dialog about sex is crucial but rare. Chapter 12 is a myth buster. It redefines "good sex" and attempts to influence a paradigm shift away from performance and "outcome" focus to one of intimate pleasure and closeness in whatever form that takes.

Chapter 13 details some sexual patterns common to many survivors of trauma, describing the behaviors, the underlying beliefs and their origins, and preliminary steps toward recovery.

Chapter 14 does the same for the neglect survivor, describing sexual behavior patterns, the core beliefs beneath them, and how to proceed toward healing the individual and the couple.

Chapter 15 begins to tie all the prior chapters together, illustrating the interplay of attachment styles, triggering, and reactivity, troubled communication, and failed empathy as they converge in repetitive, painful sexual dynamics. It suggests guidelines for identifying old patterns and creating a sexual relationship vision for the future.

Part IV is where the book becomes a how-to sex manual. Chapters 16, 17, and 18 offer stepwise preparation, and Chapter 19 a series of sequenced, hands-on practices, moving progressively from affectionate to erotic activities. Each is presented in a detailed worksheet-style format.

Chapter 20 reminds readers of the length and challenges of the healing process, emphasizing relapse-prevention practices, suggesting warning signs, and offering antidotes for common obstacles. It closes by normalizing and placing value on a commitment to work on relationship throughout life. For survivors of childhood trauma and neglect in particular, but really for everyone, intimate partnership is a work in progress requiring ongoing care and continued mindful attention.

I suggest you read the book in the order it is written because the ideas build upon what came before. I also recommend that you do the practices in sequence because they are organized in an ascending order as well. Over these decades, I have worked with numerous individuals and couples. Some of them have been heterosexual, some lesbian and gay. I have included bits and pieces of many personal stories to illustrate the concepts. All names and identifying information have been changed to protect their privacy. I have also attempted to use language that is sexually inclusive or neutral, that avoids generalization or stereotyping about gender or sexual orientation.

It is my hope that your journey will be a homecoming where you find compassion and understanding for both your own and your partner's story; you discover calm, safety, and joy in your own body and in your relationship with your partner; and your life together becomes an abode of closeness, pleasure, and delight.

# Part I

# RELATIONSHIP

## Chapter One

# IN THE BEGINNING: ATTACHMENT STYLES

When we struggle in relationship, we generally fail to see how utterly redundant and patterned our conflicts are. They might appear chaotic and unpredictable like an erupting mine field, or with the quiet stealth and rapid shifts of tropical storm clouds. In fact, however, when we look carefully, familiar outlines show up over and over again. This is good news. Rather than an incomprehensible, unstoppable destructive force, there are a handful of persistent feedback loops to understand and process.

A valuable guide to help with this comes from Attachment Theory, developed in the 1940s by infant psychiatry pioneer John Bowlby. Bowlby's research revealed that the early relationship between babies and their caregivers forms the template for relationship that persists through the lifespan. When examining the patterned relationship dynamics in our own lives, attachment theory helps bring into focus and make sense out of confounding behaviors and reactions. It might even contribute to patience and compassion for ourselves and our partners. Bowlby's theory has evolved with history and with the progress of neuroscience. We now know much about the physiological underpinnings of attachment and also that the brain can continue to grow and change throughout our lives.

## THE THREE ORIGINAL ATTACHMENT STYLES

Bowlby identified three attachment styles, and a fourth was added later. What follows is a brief overview of the styles. Do you recognize yourself in one of the styles? Do you recognize your partner? You may not remember much about your original attachment experiences; after all, the most formative occur when we are less than a year old. The intent here is not to argue the facts about what happened or to point a blaming finger at parents but simply to understand ourselves better.

## The Lucky Ones: The Securely Attached

The first of the attachment styles is the Securely Attached. These children are the lucky ones. (For brevity, and also because in Bowlby's day it was the nearly unanimous norm, I will refer to the caregiver as the mother. Of course we now know that in most ways another caregiver can fill the same role and functions.) The securely attached child has a mother who is essentially present. When the baby emits a signal, the mother sees and hears. She may mirror the child's communication or sound, "Oh you are wet, or cold or hungry," whatever the case may be. She responds in good time with what is needed, a blanket, a bottle, a diaper, or a hug. The child's distress is relatively short lived, and the baby has the experience "my feelings matter," "I will be taken care of," "I am safe."

As the securely attached child grows older and learns to crawl and walk, the mother continues to stay near. Because she is attentive and present, it is safe to explore the world, so the securely attached child is free to venture forth and exercise curiosity. If there is a moment's doubt about what is unfamiliar, the child can look back and, seeing that Mama is there, can either run back to her for reassurance or feel supported in continuing to roam. "I can check this out because Mama has my back."

Feeling supported lends a sense of confidence, and these children are confident. They learn not only that their feelings matter, which conveys to them that *they* matter, but they also learn that relationships can be a supportive and reliable resource. "I can count on Mama" and "I have value" follow this child and generalize to other people and other relationships as the child grows older. Feeling loveable, making friends, and expressing emotions and needs will feel natural and safe for this growing child and later adult. Relationship will be much easier.

Interestingly, in the best case scenario of these mother-infant pairs, the percentage of the time that this good mother is accurately attuned and responsive to her child's signals and needs is 30 percent! The rest of the time is an endless dance of rupture and repair, rupture and repair. So this means, even in the best case of possible worlds, we strive not for perfection, but for good repair skills. John Gottman, the leading contemporary marriage researcher, emphasizes this same point. If we hone good repair skills, we can recreate or create something akin to secure attachment even if we were not so fortunate as to start out with it.

## Push and Pull: The Anxious Ambivalent

For innumerable reasons, a mother's attention and responsiveness may be erratic. She may have postpartum depression and be functioning poorly; she may have too many other kids to give good attention to this newborn; she may have a troubled marriage in which she is left alone to parent or may even be brutalized by her partner; she may be physically sick, disabled, or mentally ill. She may have her own trauma. For whatever reason, when this baby emits a signal, the mother responds only *sometimes*. For an infant in the crib crying, whether it is because of hunger, a dirty diaper, fear, or loneliness, waiting alone in distress in the empty room and having no one come feels like dying. Having a mother who comes sometimes and sometimes not instills a sense of uncertainty and wordless terror. "I cannot count on her. Will this be the time that she takes care of me? Or will this be the time when I am alone, wet and freezing for hours?" (Of course these are not clearly articulated thoughts. The infant brain is not yet nearly developmentally capable of such complex cognitions, nor is the cerebral equipment required for autobiographical memory of such experiences.)

The result of the uncertainty is a gnawing anxiety about Mama's comings and goings. When she does come, the child wants to grab onto her for dear life and not let her go, because it is not clear when or even if she will ever come back. When she goes away, it may be devastating. "Will she ever return?" So the child might be scared, enraged, or inconsolable when she leaves. When Mama returns, however, although the child is relieved, it may take quite a while for the baby to calm down and accept a hug. The agony or terror of her absence makes it just too dangerous to reconnect. And this uncertainty is pervasive. The child is too young to wonder in words but has the experience, "Do my feelings matter at all?" "Am I worth anything at all?" "If I can't count on Mama, who can I count on, ever?"

My client Lucy had a devoted partner Eric who truly loved her. When he went on a business trip for a day or two, she would be furious, even though it was not his choice and he was off earning money for their family. During his absence, she would not even pick up the phone when he called. When he came home, it would sometimes take days for her to settle down and accept him again. Of course he was very hurt and annoyed, and her feelings made no sense to him. What had he done to deserve this?

When Lucy was an infant and throughout her childhood, her mother was often sick and would disappear for long stretches of time to bed in her darkened bedroom and sometimes to the hospital. For periods of time, Mama might be healthy and they would have fun and be close. Other times, even when she was around, Lucy's mother might be distracted and distant, lost in her world of pain, weakness, and despair. Lucy grew up feeling uncertain. All children imagine they are the center of the universe and interpret experience through that lens. When she was small, she was sure her mother's absence and inattention were because of something about *her*. "I am ugly, unlovable, bad, worthless, dumb, unwanted," Lucy concluded. She grew up feeling poorly about herself and very insecure.

Of course Eric and others were offended that she assumed the worst about their comings and goings or perceived rejection so readily in whatever they did. She would get so angry that she often ended up pushing people right out of her life and then feeling desperately lonely. When I, her therapist, went away for a conference or vacation, she felt as if I were abandoning *her*, going away to get away from *her*. She still had the infantile belief that whatever happened was caused by or about her. For Lucy, the world of relationship was a living hell, until she was lucky enough to find a partner who would work on these patterns with her. Of course, the work was challenging and lengthy for them!

## OUT OF SIGHT, OUT OF MIND: THE AVOIDANTLY ATTACHED

Admittedly I am not fond of the label Bowlby assigned to this group. To me, "avoidance" smacks of behavior someone might do on purpose. Frankly, I just don't see these children and later adults that way. Avoidant attachment is the beginning of what I view as the spectrum of neglect. The "avoidant" child is far too often and too long left alone from an early age. These babies learn early that it is pointless to cry because no one ever comes. So from the beginning they are of necessity self-sufficient, and before they are even aware of it, they operate out of the belief "I have to do it all myself." They have no reason to think of other people as resources for them.

In our culture of rugged individualism, self-sufficiency may seem like an asset, yet as a species we are wired for relationship, and the avoidant person misses out on the basics of how to relate. Often when these children grow up and reflect on their childhoods, they recount a story that seems vacant of other humans. They might speak of pets, activities and interests, with any stories of human relationships strangely absent.

In the early days of my own marriage, we struggled through periods of chronic conflict and disconnection. After a painful episode, my husband, a quintessential avoidant, would log onto his computer and go back to work. I would stew for hours or days about our disagreement. My anguish was compounded by his ability to completely put it out of his mind. I remember one particularly painful upheaval at the beginning of a workday. As I was about to head out for work, I grimly said to him, "I bet as soon as I leave this house, you will completely forget about me and not think of me at all until I darken the door tonight!" Matter-of-factly he responded, "You know what? You're right!" And I was. The avoidant, the child of neglect, learns early to compartmentalize and split off feelings about others in order to survive.

The avoidantly attached may be fairly effective in the world, having learned early on to be independent. They may also have a deep streak of global anger, even entitlement, from having been expected to fend for themselves. And for all their competence, they might be strangely clueless about social life, having grown up in something like a social desert. More about them later when we explore the experience of neglect.

## THE DILEMMA WITHOUT SOLUTION: THE DISORGANIZED DISORIENTED

In subsequent post–Bowlby years, as attachment theory continued to grow and evolve, a team of researchers at UC Berkeley headed by psychologist/ researcher Mary Main added a fourth attachment style: the disorganized disoriented. Main characterized these children as being caught in a "dilemma without solution." Many traumatized children and later adults relate in this style. For these children, a parent or important loved one and a brutal abuser or tyrant are the very same: the source of sustenance and comfort and the source of terror and pain are the same person. The child both reaches for and recoils from that person at the same time. There is no safe way to relate. The resulting behavior is a kind of wobble and then freeze state where the child wavers between reaching and withdrawal, does nothing, collapses into inertia, or zones out.

In one couple I worked with, Lisa would chronically shut down and seem to vanish rather than attempt to talk about her feelings. Her partner Chris would get exasperated and angry when instead of talking through a difficulty as Chris would have liked to, Lisa would say a few clipped, often incoherent words and then quickly say, "I'm done." It was too dangerous for Lisa to attempt communication. She would require hours or even days to calm down and thaw. Chris felt impatient, frustrated, often superior, and also hurt, lonely, and abandoned, wishing they could *really* talk.

## MAKING USE OF ATTACHMENT THEORY

So how is any of this of use to us in our relationships? A fundamental key to resolving relationship problems when there is a trauma/neglect background is deeply "getting" a fundamental concept: "It's not about me." In my own case, the idea that my partner could completely forget about me for an entire day after a painful interlude could devastate me. It could confirm my age-old belief about myself, coming from my own attachment history, that I am invisible and I don't matter. Learning that my beliefs about my own worthlessness predated this relationship, that my partner did not do that to me, and learning that he survived his childhood by putting important people and painful interactions with them completely out of mind, helped both of us to see more clearly and in present time. I could feel compassion and sadness for a little boy who was so alone. I could quiet the part of myself that was so insulted, incensed, or hurt by being "forgotten." Not overnight, but over time, it helped us. Do you see anything in any of the styles that would be of use to you?

# Chapter Two

## THE PRACTICE OF EMPATHY: WHAT'S WRONG WITH THE GOLDEN RULE?

The child of trauma or neglect lives in a desolate and lonely world. For the most part there is no one there orienting or teaching this child about life. So she or he wanders, constantly struggling to figure it all out. Of course, that young brain is ill equipped for such a task. One mistaken conclusion that these children and later adults will reach is that "everyone feels as I do." Chocolate is so delicious! *Everyone* loves it. We only know our own experience and we thus deduce that our experience is universal. We may take our assumptions so for granted that like the air we breathe, we don't even notice them.

I woke up dramatically to this fact early in my relationship with my partner. Always a person who loves any occasion for gift giving, I was excited to celebrate his birthday shortly after we got together. I take great pleasure and pride in coming up with abundant, thoughtful, creative, and generous gifts. Anticipating my new partner's birthday, I went all out, thinking of a number of what I thought were really special things that he might like and that would express how I felt about him. I carefully wrapped them all, and I could hardly wait to surprise him.

When the day finally came, and I showed up with my Santa-like load of packages, *I* had a surprise. I had expected my partner would feel delighted, flattered, thrilled, and loved by my abundant show of affection. That is how *I* would have felt, so of course he would feel as I would. But he did not! His face had an odd expression, a mixture of fear, suspicion, and anger. Clearly he was not pleased. I was shocked. I figured there must be something wrong with him. What kind of person would not be happy with these sumptuous gifts? I was hurt. I had put tremendous thought and effort into planning; I had spent a lot of my hard-earned money and then painstakingly prepared each package. I felt unappreciated, baffled, and insulted. We proceeded to have our first fight. What a disappointment that was.

What I later learned was my partner's bitter and painful childhood experience around gifts. His mother routinely gave him things that *she* liked or wanted instead of bothering to find out what *he* might like or want; she gave him what *she* wanted to give him or what she thought he *should* want. "It was all about her," he explained to me. "Her gifts to me were little more than ways for her to gratify *herself*. And then I was supposed to be so grateful . . . " It had all been a colossal nightmare for him and no fun at all. Of course when he saw me coming with armloads of gifts, he would be suspicious: "What are you trying to get?" Or feel used: "You are just getting *yourself* off!" It did make sense that those would be his reactions.

It took me a long time to "get it," however. I continued to believe that I was "right," that something was "wrong" with a person who did not enjoy gifts. I set out to enlighten him, to teach him to be more like me. Needless to say, he was a less-than-enthusiastic student. We struggled with gifts for a long time. He insisted that the perfect gift for him was one simple item that he selected himself, preferably not expensive and not a surprise. I felt thwarted and deprived of the opportunity to show my "love." I was devastated and judgmental about "not being received" until I learned an essential relationship principle: If you want to say "I love you" to your partner (or anyone, for that matter), find out what says I love you to *him* or *her*, and do that! If I give you what I would want, what I want to give you, or what I think you *should* want, I will more than likely fail to touch your heart. The Golden Rule, "Do unto others as you would have them do unto you," is a good start. But with all due respect, it falls short.

True empathy is the ability to truly see through the eyes of the other, even when the view is vastly different from my own. We need not agree. I need not adopt my partner's point of view and be like him. Rather, I must compassionately understand and respect his point of view. It makes perfect sense for him to feel as he does in light of his experience. With that respectful understanding, I stop trying to turn him into a replica of me.

It also took a while to establish that although I could accept my partner's wishes for *his* birthday, I had very different ones for mine! His challenge was one of learning that what for him had been a vehicle of coercion and control *could* in fact be an expression of generosity and love, at least on my birthday. This was no small feat for us.

Particularly difficult is an empathic response when the point of view I am being asked to understand involves a gross distortion of me or my intentions!

To look through my partner's eyes and see his picture of my behavior as self-centered and manipulative was a tall order at best. It took a long time of adamantly reminding myself "this is *not* about me!" Unfortunately, it is often the case that my partner's *particular* distortion of me or my behavior strikes a nerve in my own history, making compassion and even clear thinking all the more elusive. But more about this later.

## EMPATHY AND SAFETY

In the course of my years as a couples therapist, I gradually noticed that virtually all of the couples who came through my doors seemed to wrangle with the same sticky question. They might think their problem was parenting or sex, money or communication, but it really boiled down to this: Do I have to give up me to have you? Or do I have to give you up to really be myself? Might it ever be possible for each of us to be ourselves, unique, distinct, and connected? It seems a tall if not unattainable order.

Most of us learn from our parents "Be like us, do as we do." That is "good." If you do something else, that is "bad" or "wrong." So we come to understand that "like is good" and different means someone is "wrong." In many trauma and neglect families, the cost of being different was dangerously high. It might range from being physically punished, rejected, hated, abandoned, or later disinherited, to a more subtle and deadening drone of being chronically "corrected," criticized, humiliated, and shamed for being different.

Being free to be oneself is as precious as life itself. Being stifled, thwarted, or squeezed into someone else's mold is a kind of living death by strangulation. Children of such childhoods go into relationship (or avoid relationship) dreading that this experience will be repeated.

Many partnerships get stymied with each individual trying to convince the other that "mine is the right way" or "my view is the 'truth,'" as if there were only one way or one truth. I have come to the conclusion that there are in fact precious few absolute truths. Almost everything we think and believe is subjective and subject to personal interpretation. For me to believe that I have "the truth" is arrogant at best. The epitome of safety is the knowledge that I am in a relationship that assumes this: We each live in our own world and have our own unique perceptions and feelings. If you can understand my feelings and I yours, and we can coexist with the contrast, we can have peace and harmony. I can relax in the knowing that I can live rather than fear the living death of alienation and coercion. This is no small thing, and is foundational also to successful and loving sexuality. For many of the traumatized, this unquestionable knowledge is precisely what makes the vulnerability inherent in sexual intimacy impossible.

We will have much to say about safety. For now, take a moment and think about it: How safe is it to be openly different in my partnership? How respectful, accepting, and even curious am I about the ways my partner is different from me? How able am I, really, to see through my partner's eyes, walk in my partner's shoes, and even empathically hear my partner's experience of me?

## Chapter Three

# DON'T GET ME WRONG! HD COMMUNICATION

When high-definition (HD) television first hit the appliance stores some years ago, I remember walking around marveling at the giant screens. The pictures were so razor sharp, the colors so astonishingly vivid, I felt as if I were under water swimming with the life-size fish or actually in the office with Tony Soprano and his therapist. It was as clear and intense as being right there in the story. This is the model for HD communication: crystalline clarity that truly facilitates a swim in the other's reality. It is old news that how couples communicate can make all the difference between a relaxed, harmonious, close relationship and a nightmare. What may be less obvious is that to a large extent, we each have our own private dictionary and the same words can have an infinite number of wildly or mildly different definitions. HD communication is an effort to sharpen our focus and learn the language of the other so that when we speak, we are in fact on the same page.

Sadly, many of us know too well that miscommunication can explode the mood with lightning speed and shocking suddenness. It can dramatically contribute to a feeling that the relationship is not safe. If one or both partners are on chronic alert for a verbal or nonverbal bombshell, there is no peace. Gradually we may observe waning desire to spend time together or confusion about why one or both of us avoids being alone together. Why would anyone choose to attempt to relax in a climate reminiscent of a battle zone or one's embattled childhood?

And what are these bombshells? In general, they are perceived insults or threats, with an emphasis on "perceived." We now know that a gift, or virtually anything, can be perceived as an insult or threat, depending upon one's world view. So there are infinite possibilities for how any communication, be it verbal or otherwise, can be interpreted, misinterpreted, or somehow completely garbled. I take as given that living in different worlds to some extent, we each have our own personal lexicon with our very own idiosyncratic meanings for words and terms and our own private slang. I know I do. There are words and expressions that I will make a long detour around the linguistic block to avoid uttering and that I cringe to hear. And I see this daily in others, who may or may not be aware of their bias. I have become a bullish watchdog for precise speech, self-aware facial expression, and mindful body language to begin to create a demilitarized communication zone and ultimately an environment inviting to intimacy.

You may be saying, "Our relationship is not like that. We don't fight, we barely talk at all." This may be but a variation on the same theme. Is it safe to talk to one another? What are the chances of being understood? Or would it be pointless, painful, or just too much effort? Even if none of these possibilities fits, I suggest giving some thought to the concepts in this chapter. Self-expression is foundational to attachment and relatedness right from the beginning of life. How our earliest signals are responded to or not is instrumental in how we think of ourselves and others.

What follows is a mini-handbook of principles of communication distilled from a voluminous reading of the literature, thousands of hours of therapy sessions, and an honest accounting of success and failure in my own communication life. To be sure, it is not exhaustive (although it might be exhausting!). Rather, it is intended to provide a framework.

## A BIG BANG: WHENEVER THERE IS A BIG CHARGE OF EMOTION, INVARIABLY THERE IS AN ANTECEDENT FROM CHILDHOOD

This principle is often controversial. If I am righteously hurt or angry, of course I prefer to believe that *you* did this to me. I'd rather *not* believe that I am living in the past or somehow "to blame" myself. This is not to say that one partner never says something that hurts or affronts the other, but rather, the magnitude of the reaction is what is telling. Harville Hendrix, the founder of Imago Relationship Therapy, describes it as "stepping on my sore toe." Granted, you did step on my toe, and it hurt, but the vulnerability was already there. And if the vulnerability lurked quietly and undisclosed, my lurching pain reaction might appear exaggerated, even feigned or manipulative. That in itself can incite a volley of miscommunication.

Toby's childhood experience was to feel chronically unheard. "Nobody listened to me or cared what I had to say. Nobody ever remembered what I had said." Toby's partner Jan was somewhat hard of hearing and sometimes did not register that Toby had spoken. Sometimes Jan would say, "What did you say?" and Toby would go angrily silent and refuse to say it again. Granted, sometimes Jan was not directing quality attention toward Toby; but sometimes it was truly an issue of not being able to hear. At those times, Jan felt that Toby was mean, impatient, and unsympathetic and walked away thinking, "Fine, I don't want to talk to *you* either."

The point is that the fact that many of us would be annoyed by constantly having to repeat ourselves, becoming furious to the point of not wanting to speak anymore, suggests some prior injury that would make a seemingly innocuous or minor expression or action into a very big deal.

Most couples have a handful of repeating cycles that rear up over and over again. It is helpful to identify your own vulnerabilities so you can work on becoming less reactive and so you can help your partner understand why you react so extremely. It also helps to better understand your partner's vulnerabilities so you can stay off that toe and contribute to an environment that is more peaceful for both of you.

What are your Big Bang communication patterns? What are your own communication sore spots? Can you locate their origins in your past?

## FILLING IN THE BLANKS

Children of trauma and neglect do grow up in desolation. In general, communication in the childhood home is not the best. The nature of trauma is that the brain and body of the organism become hyperalert and watchful for signals of danger in an endless self-protective effort. Children of trauma may become vigilant students of the minds and behaviors of others, often honing and relying on exquisitely sensitive powers of intuition. Children of neglect may live in a world of echoing silence. If no one is talking to them, they may make up their own explanations for what they see and experience, attempting to make sense out of the world. Both of these kids may become quite skilled and effective at "reading" or analyzing others' feelings and motivations. Some may not be as good as they think they are, but they are definitely highly practiced. Some may even go on to become therapists, believing they have been trained by their whole lives.

In relationship, these talents can cut both ways. They may make for a high level of psychological acuity or radar-like sensitivity and an awareness of the power and importance of emotions. In turn, they may manifest in a conscious or unconscious arrogance of assuming, "I know what is going on with you, even if you don't tell me, perhaps even better than you do!" It can evolve into what I call "filling in the blanks."

Filling in the blanks is when I translate the unspoken or unclearly spoken message in my own way instead of inquiring of the speaker. For example, I might feel rejected, interpreting your watching television with headphones as a way to shut me out. You might be using the headphones with the intention of being considerate, knowing I don't like the noise of TV car racing. Rather than finding out from you what your motivation is, I get my feelings hurt (by the explanation that I made up) and leave the house feeling sorry for myself. You find yourself feeling annoyed and like you just can't win with me.

Admittedly, this principle can be a hard sell. Not infrequently have I met with ire when attempting to teach it for appearing to steal or negate a gift of intuition that in the past may have been life saving. I do understand the feeling. Yet like many other childhood adaptations, it doesn't work effectively anymore.

In general, we all tend to fill in the blanks in the direction of the negative, and we all tend to fill in the blanks through the lens of our own childhood experience. Don't guess, don't assume you know. Rather than filling in the blanks, tell your partner what you are feeling and check out the accuracy of your perception. You may be very surprised—and, not infrequently, quite relieved!

Another variation on filling in the blanks is "I know what you're going to say . . . ": in effect, having the conversation alone without actually even finding out what the other was going to say. I call this "running both sides of the relationship" because you are effectively being yourself and the other person, too. I had a friend who would chronically do that with me. She'd say, "I know what you're thinking," and unveil some unsavory judgment of her that would never have crossed my mind. Not only was she presumptuous, but she effectively erased me from the equation by being both of us, leaving me to wonder why I was sitting there. I was offended by the obnoxious thoughts that she attributed to me, so I might end up annoyed with her even if I didn't start out that way.

What tendencies do you have to fill in the blanks? What are the themes of the fictions you concoct about your partner's nonverbal or incompletely verbalized communications? Do you recognize those themes from your past?

## STAYING IN YOUR OWN YARD

A short hop from filling in the blanks is the concept of "staying in your own yard." I noticed early on in my work with trauma and neglect couples how often I found myself saying, particularly to the neglect survivor, "Talk about you. Talk about you" as I interrupted a long and detailed analytical description of the other partner. The message of the neglect experience is "there is no me," and the child becomes very focused on the parent who seems to be the one with both existence and power. More about this later. For now, suffice it to say that too often partners are quick to second-guess, psychoanalyze, and pontificate about the behavior, motivations, or character of the other. Where earlier in the relationship the attention and interest might be flattering, it rapidly comes to feel disrespectful and intrusive, not to mention inaccurate.

Sandy says, "You're just avoiding sex with me to get back at me. You're mad at me for not making more money and for not being able to take you on the kind of vacations you like. So you punish me by withholding sex. You're passive-aggressive and you don't care a bit about my feelings!" This wordy diatribe inspires an angry, defensive response from Dale and a frosty withdrawal from the "conversation." Replete with accusations and "you statements," Sandy's speech effectively communicates nothing. Dale feels attacked and more disconnected—certainly less like having sex!

So what would be a communication from Sandy's own yard? That would be the old "I statements," information about Sandy and Sandy's feelings. Granted, it requires more vulnerability to speak about oneself than to size up the other. Yet that is precisely what is both communicative and ultimately connecting. Sandy might say, "I'm sad and tired and mad that we don't have sex. I feel rejected and hurt that something so important to me is just plain missing from our life." Although not cheerful, that might be something that Dale could hear and that might give rise to an exchange rather than an argument or a cool détente.

By the way, speculating about your partner's or anyone else's feelings will make you very anxious, especially as we tend to imagine the worst. Identifying and naming your own feelings, however, is inherently calming. In fact, there is research showing that the simple act of naming the emotion at the moment it is being felt quiets the nervous system: another incentive for staying in your own yard.

How well do you know your own yard and feelings? How quick are you to rush over and critique or landscape your partner's?

## BUT YOU SAID . . .

The hypervigilance of trauma and neglect seems to cement in memory some of the most frightening or painful utterances from important others. They might echo in the mind for years and decades, even becoming part of one's self-concept. Unfortunately, partners might be inclined to similarly immortalize each other's words on large or small subjects. One partner might still be stewing about something the other said long after the speaker has forgotten or had a change of heart about what was expressed.

Imago therapist Maya Kollman introduced me to a Native American quote that has become immortal with me: "If you think you know me, you've stopped my growth in your presence." This means, if you hold me to something I said

20 years ago, or last week, or even 5 minutes ago, you close off the possibility that I might be changing and growing in our relationship. I strongly encourage partners to be ever updating their files rather than assuming that what was stated some time in the past will endure as the eternal truth.

Are there statements that your partner made decades ago that remain wedged in your craw? What are they? When is the last time you checked to find out their current status?

## NEEDS VS. FEELINGS; QUESTIONS VS. STATEMENTS

These are smaller points, which is why I have grouped them together. In general, I recommend speaking in terms of feelings instead of *wants* or *needs*. This is a personal bias. I know there are whole communication systems based in expressing needs. Many children of trauma and neglect lived in families where there was not enough to go around, either literally or figuratively. If one wanted or needed, that might pit him or her against the others and the others' wants and needs in this zero-sum game. Speaking in terms of needs may sound either polarizing (my needs or yours, who will win?) Or it may sound coercive, because for many the needs or wants of the parents were delivered as orders.

"I need the house to be tidy." Or "When the house is tidy, I feel calmer." Which sounds more inviting to you?

I also recommend making statements instead of asking questions. Questions can be a veiled way of hovering in your partner's yard. Bruce could easily start a fight by asking "Are you mad at me?" Lisa would be offended by the question or annoyed by the unsavory accusation. Then she might in fact *get* angry, sick and tired of being misunderstood or viewed as a rager. If Bruce had said, "I feel such distance between us. I'm not sure how to read your silence and your serious expression," it might have lead to more connection instead of less.

## DON'T BE GREEDY; YOU CAN ONLY HAVE HALF!

I will say this over and over because it is very important to me: This is a *no-blame* paradigm. Rarely if ever is only one partner at fault for a difficulty. In general, traumatized people are inclined to explain the world's woes as their own fault. Many were overtly blamed as children even for their own abuse. In many relationships there is a designated "problem child" and a designated "endurer" or saintlike "suffering spouse." I don't buy this division of labor. The problem child defaults quickly to self-blame. The endurer agrees. I call this "the grand collusion." I will say to the self-blamer on a regular basis, "Don't be greedy; you can only have half!" as we attempt to disarm these roles and uncover the true dynamics.

As I said earlier, if there is one partner consistently viewed to be at fault, that person generally gets both all the blame and all the help, while the other partner disappears, freed not only of responsibility but also of any attention or assistance, either. What are the roles in your partnership?

## TOO MANY WORDS!

Finally, I frequently hear myself interrupting couples and saying, "Too many words, too many words." We've all seen the comedy routines with two people who do not speak the same language failing in their attempt to understand each other and be understood. They continue their effort by repeating themselves only louder, as if that will help to get the message across. In a similar way, I observe partners attempting to be understood with lengthy explanations illustrated with a litany of metaphors and examples. The result is the listener feeling drowned in words and the speaker's point lost in the sea of words. More than one example may very well elicit defensiveness or rebuttal about what "actually" happened. And metaphor, while an elegant ingredient for poetry, often injects ambiguity, vagueness, and distance in personal dialog. In general, fewer words that closely hug the main point carry much more potency and are much more likely to be "gotten."

Can you make your point simply and just once? Or do you feel the need to give a long oratory to be understood? Why?

Some clients complained to me in fatigued frustration, "Too many rules! I can't begin to speak!" I am convinced you can say whatever it is you need to say, staying in your own yard, speaking about your own feelings, concisely and respectfully. What is required is mindfulness, intention, and practice. Clearly there is much to say about HD communication! I shall attempt to heed my own advice, however, knowing we will cover more about it along the way.

## Chapter Four

# CHIAROSCURO: THE PLAY OF SHADOW AND LIGHT

Growing up in a landscape of trauma and neglect is a childhood of lonely bleakness. Children are of course exquisitely sensitive to the presence, absence, and moods of their important others. Even parents who are not angry or terrifying have a profound impact on the vulnerable child. Attachment researchers studying infants' relationships with their caregivers did one famous experiment known as the "still face." The mothers in the study were instructed to hold their faces vacant of any expression for a period of one or two minutes. The films are heartbreaking. Invariably the young child gazing up at an expressionless or blank visage of Mama would first break into instantaneous cries of confusion and distress, then immediately desperately attempt anything to make her smile or react somehow.

The infant brain develops in resonance. If there is nobody there with whom to resonate, or if the essential other is distant, disconnected, frightening, or frightened, what then? These early experiences profoundly shape the outlook of these small, developing people, and the world appears cold and dark. If the mothers and fathers are traumatized themselves, sick, depressed, or immensely stressed in the present, they may appear tense, stern, or angry much of the time, which may then be the backdrop or accompaniment for daily home life.

Do you find you react strongly to your partner's grim expression or a hint of anger in your partner's face? Do you feel anxious when your partner has a faraway look? Do you begin to "tap dance," attempt to be "perfect," become a clown, a hypochondriac, or a brat? These are all understandable adaptations Do you feel angry or abandoned when there is silence or conversation is sparse? Is there a poverty of smiles, laughter, and affection between you? Do you praise or acknowledge each other? Or is the cold emptiness of childhood trauma and neglect recreating itself in your adult home? It would not be surprising if it were.

## DEPRESSION COMES WITH THE TERRITORY

The diagnosis of Post-Traumatic Stress Disorder includes depression as part of the symptom picture. Living in the wake of one overwhelming episode and in anticipation of the next is an unstable, joyless existence. Many adults with histories of trauma and neglect have few memories of joy and levity and may even be hard pressed to define what these words mean to them. They may have grown up in a sea of seriousness and downplayed or questioned whether pleasure even had any intrinsic value at all. Marcy grew up with two parents who had survived the Holocaust and for years believed that amusement and play were trivial and superficial. She equated suffering with heroism or worthiness and felt embarrassed and petty for even wanting to have a good time. Some children of trauma and neglect were so busy getting through the days, either trying to be safe or to master the art of self-reliance, that they never had the opportunity to discover their own passions, interests, and delight. So life is not much fun.

## THE FIVE-TO-ONE RATIO

The famous relationship researcher John Gottman has spent some 40 years painstakingly collecting data about what makes for successful partnerships, effectively shaping the seeming mystery and chaos of couplehood into science. Gottman has statistically identified specific behaviors, skills, and practices that predict lasting, satisfying relationships and, in turn, what patterns of action and/or oversight portend separation and divorce. One key finding, now central in my work, is Gottman's Five-to-One Ratio. The data revealed that in order for a relationship to remain stable—not to improve and not to backslide but to just stay steady—the ratio of positive to negative must be five to one! That is, five smiles for every frown; five compliments for every complaint; five acknowledgments for every failure to notice just to break even! This is the formula for generic couples. In couples where there is a history of trauma and neglect, where the scale is tipped in the direction of sadness and fear, boosting up the positive is an even more fundamental necessity. Unwittingly, negativity may readily be endemic, like ambient air, when there is depression and anxiety on board. We may not even be aware of our humorlessness, sarcasm, irritability, and criticism. What would you say is the positive-to-negative ratio in your relationship?

## APPRECIATION

It is amazing how easy it is to turn the tide by infusing the relationship with positive input. Gottman is quick to point out that having a cushion or savings account of accumulated positives lends resilience and inoculates the connection. If I am accustomed to hearing lots of good things from my partner, the occasional gripe does not sting so sharply. When I am constantly met with reminders and evidence of how I fall short, I will feel defeated, defensive, and probably less inspired to please.

One very simple way to bump up the positive is by expressing appreciation. There are two categories of appreciation: recognition and gratitude. Recognition would be, "I appreciate what a difficult day you've had and how hard your job is." Gratitude would be, "I appreciate how hard you work to bring home money for our family, especially when you have such a hard job and long commute. Thank you!" Both kinds of appreciation add to your reserve of positives. I am, however, partial to gratitude because it is more personal.

It is almost a joke in my office. No couple gets out my door without ending the session with two rounds of appreciation of each other, no matter what kind of session it has been. When you are hurt and angry, appreciations are harder to express. And that is precisely when they are most needed. I believe that appreciation benefits the appreciat*or* even more than the appreciat*ee*. Sometimes one partner may be so dismayed or disgusted with the other as to begin to wonder with humiliation, "What is wrong with *me* for putting up with this?" Expressing appreciation might be a reminder of something good, of why I am with this person. It might even make me feel better about myself!

## YOUR WIFE IS A GENIUS!

I remember a time in my marriage when it seemed my partner just did not notice the good things I did. Feeling invisible, hurt, and angry, I would pout, punishing him for his "insensitivity" or "obliviousness." Then I discovered that with humor and gentleness, I could toot my own horn just a bit. "What a good cat I am!" Or "Your wife is a genius!" As long as I did so without bitterness, competition, or reprimand, I could point out my contributions and maybe get the acknowledgment by fishing. Perhaps not my first choice, of course; I would have been happier if he had noticed my heroic taking out of all the trash, compost, *and* recycling without prompting or figuring out how to get my computer to work myself instead of yet again interrupting him to do it. But helping him to notice was a lot more constructive than my old pouting routine. I think ultimately it helped him to be more observant of my big and little positives.

## DO YOU HAVE TIME FOR A HUG?

Physical affection is another form of expression that can profoundly affect the positive climate. A hug, a warm hand, or a head rub might be worth a thousand words. Surprises and little treats are also good. I always say flowers are a quick and sure way to raise your five-to-one ratio. Compliments, even good news, are constructive inputs into the account. Remember, you will be doing more than contributing to your relationship's sustainability. You will also be combating your own depressive tendency and your partner's too! And if you have children, it will certainly brighten up the environment in which they grow up, making it different from the one you grew up in.

What would you say is your current quotient of positivity? What might you be willing to do about it? Would you be willing to go ahead and start giving more, even not knowing if your partner will too?

## TIME TO "KVETCH"

Drew and Alice felt perennially tense around each other. Both felt defensive and on guard for large and small complaints that seemed to sprout like an infestation of toxic weeds choking out the daylight in the environment between them. We decided to reserve a specific time each day for complaining. It was a radical experiment, and here is what we discovered: By containing their negative remarks until the designated time, they not only became capable of containing the negative, but they also found themselves increasingly mindful of their *own* negativity when before they had been so focused on each other's. And they kept the vicinity around their kids free of barbs and blame.

Of course there was a hitch. We required that they uphold the five-to-one ratio. So when they came to the "kvetch" sessions with their carefully saved-up gripes, they had to counterbalance each negative with five expressions of positive feeling: appreciation, compliments, or acknowledgments. With the busyness of their days, they felt able to allot only half an hour per day for grumble time, so they agreed to limit themselves to two complaints plus the requisite 10 appreciations each. That would easily consume the session. They discovered that many of their negative feelings were not all that important to express; and they found the climate in the household brightened considerably with this new practice, which came to feel increasingly like a game. Try it!

## Chapter Five

# MEN AND WOMEN: IS THERE A DIFFERENCE?

On a fairly regular basis I receive e-mails from far and wide with messages like, "The articles on your website made me cry. I read every single one. I had no idea anyone else feels the way I do." "I thought I was the only one. Maybe I am not as crazy as I imagined." "Maybe there is a way out of this agony . . ." The writers find a whiff of relief or a ray of hope in the generalizations. There is some sort of comfort in discovering that what had seemed so random, unique, and outside the norm might be part of some larger constellation that makes some kind of sense.

Children growing up alone in a world of fear, pain, and shame generally do not have the luxury of explanations and definitions. Some later discover theory or science, but many do not. The conclusion they ultimately reach is, "There is something wrong with *me*," "I simply don't get along with humans," or some other self-referencing system of logic. This makes sense in a desolate world where there is no other clear reference point. Small children by nature believe that they are the center of the universe, and somehow all events in their little world are their own handiwork or their fault. In a silent world of isolation, these beliefs can live on.

That is one reason why I find it useful and interesting to visit different paradigms, theories, and organizing systems as alternative lenses through which to observe and interpret reality. I've already introduced attachment theory, which I find a tremendously illuminating model for understanding behavior and relationship patterns. Other vistas come from science.

As you will see, I am an enthusiastic student of the body and brain and how neuroscience bears on the complex world of trauma, neglect, relationship, and sex. Another interesting avenue to consider is anthropology, "evolutionary psychology," albeit controversial and overly simple to some. Our intention in paying a visit to it here is not to stereotype or make cookie-cutter-like assumptions about anyone but to try on alternative, perhaps kinder templates for understanding our partners' behavior and our own.

## CONNECTION

Historically and prehistorically, women were caregivers. As a lifelong endurance athlete, I bristle at the generalization that the females of the species have tended to be smaller and weaker. Alas, even among other species, this appears to be true. And women, being the bearers of the young, were the ones designated to stay behind and care for them and the elderly while the bigger and stronger males went out to hunt or provide protection.

Where for the males, physical strength was the font of safety, the females banded together to be safe when the men were away. Their safety was in numbers and in their connection with each other. Especially with vulnerable young or old to care for, a "village" was often required to feel comfortable, secure, and effective. It is possible that this genetic tendency has persisted through the millennia, that women are more frightened of and devastated by disconnection.

Do you tend to feel fear when the connection is broken or lost or when you are alone? If your partner is a male, do you find you suffer from distance more than he does? Does it seem to you that he just does not "get" how painful this is for you? When you are worried, scared, or upset about something, do you seek refuge in relationship more than he does? Have you interpreted his tendencies to mean he doesn't "care" as much as you do or as evidence that you "don't matter"?

## SUCCESS

As mentioned above, the males were vested with the mandate to protect and to a large extent to provide. Prevailing at the hunt and at war were requisite to survival for men and their charges. Failure might amount to massacre, defeat to starvation and extinction. With such high stakes, men might place vitally high value on success—again, a gene that may live on.

In turn, loss and defeat may strike a deeper and more dramatic chord in men than in women. Carlos, an accomplished cardiologist, was struggling and battling disappointments and disrespect at work. When a project he designed was rejected and he was passed over for a promotion, he became profoundly depressed. His partner Heather responded with sympathy, to which Carlos reacted angrily. He felt humiliated, shamed, and mocked by her "pity," and then she could not understand why it was "such a big deal."

Does it feel like life and death to you whether you succeed or fail? Does it humiliate or enrage you when you are corrected or "shown up?" If your partner is female, does it seem that she just does not "get" how important this is to you?

## GETTING TO SEX: CHICKEN OR EGG?

A well-known paradoxical tangle that I encounter on a regular basis in heterosexual couples is the impasse created by her insistence, "I can't have sex with you. I don't feel a bit connected to you. Why would I want to have sex with you? You don't even talk to me!" And his retort, "I have nothing to say to you! You won't even touch me!" If women need to feel connected in order to be sexual and men need to be sexual in order to feel connected, where do we begin? Or does a frosty standoff stop all action for long periods of time?

Some couples find such "stuck places" hopelessly demoralizing, yet another dilemma without solution. Chicken or egg: How do we move beyond this?

## THE HORMONES OF MIDLIFE

One final gender challenge before we move on comes with midlife. In the big evolutionary picture, these are problems of the modern world. As recently as a century ago, the typical lifespan was such that women did not live much beyond menopause. Economic reality mandated having sizeable families to insure a sufficient labor force to be solvent and to be taken care of when one might be too old to take care of oneself. The survival mandate to be fruitful and multiply provided good reason to be sexual. Neither men nor women lived much beyond childbearing ages, so the challenges of postmenopausal sexuality and creating a monogamous sexual life that would remain interesting and lively or just plain continue for several more decades were relatively rare.

Now that we live twice as long as our grandparents did, our physiology and our relationship models require a radical updating. Culture is clumsily attempting to achieve this, but as evidenced by our persistently pathetic divorce statistics, we are not there yet.

## DO-SE-DO

Estrogen truly does fuel the caretaking instinct. It may sound horribly politically incorrect to say it, but if it appears that women are more fluent, effective, and natural providers of nurture and empathy, it is because, estrogen-aided, we are. Nature wired us to be so inclined to fulfill the mandate of preserving the species. However, at midlife, when estrogen recedes, the caretaking impulse often declines with it. This may mean that the inspiration and impulse, the intrinsic reflex and even pleasure in putting the interests of the growing and developing other first have settled.

A new wave may be starting to swell in the midlife woman, of desire to move out into the world and perhaps advance her own interests and potentials. The children being launched, she may be moved to launch herself in a new way. And she may be tired, bored, and even resentful of the many responsibilities that formerly she and her partner took for granted as hers. This shifting of intentions may be conscious or not. It may simply show itself in irritation and friction that may surprise an unwitting partner or offspring who was not aware that something had changed. She herself may feel unnerved or guilty about her own unfamiliar discontent or restlessness. This is one of the less anticipated "sequelae" of menopause. Estrogen as "mother's little helper" begins to retire.

Testosterone, in turn, powers the male instinct to slay dragons, to guard the safety of the tribe, and to "bring home the bacon," as it were. As men age and testosterone begins to recede, these impulses may begin to quiet. Men may find themselves more inclined to stay closer to home, to have a smaller, simpler world. They may feel less driven toward challenge, perhaps more toward retirement. So nature may present us with a paradoxical developmental confluence: Just as she feels free and ready to spread her wings and fly, he feels free and ready to relax by the hearth. The biochemistry of midlife presents a novel challenge.

Couples that anticipate the challenges and recognize that there may be extra work to do in the middle years to "re-sync" the relationship and head them off will be at an advantage. Couples who were not forewarned and find themselves more at odds than they may be accustomed to may be relieved to find it is a normative hiccup of the life cycle or can be if approached together.

Do you seem to want to realize your own individual potential more now that you may have more choice about it? Does your partner seem to want to function more independently than in the past? Do you prefer to stay close to home, relax, value domesticity more than in the past? Does your partner seem more of a homebody than you remember? How might you approach these changes and stay connected?

## SUMMING UP

The point of this chapter is not to make hard and fast rules about gender! Of course this paradigm leaves out the indelible stamp of culture that also has everything to do with gene expression. Gender roles and stereotypes have been in economical, political, and sociological upheaval certainly over the last 50 years, even the past 100. So the gender lens is far from static, and I do not mean to be reductionist here. Rather, my fascination with integration and examining relationship from any accessible angle compels me to consider this view also, for whatever it is worth. I think of the toy kaleidoscopes we played with as kids. Squinting through the peephole at one end brings into view a panoply of colors and shapes. Turning the focus ring on the column of the kaleidoscope, or with some of them shaking it up, changes not just the colors and shapes but also the various patterns they configure together. When we struggle in relationship, we might be viewing problems from a tightly circumscribed perspective. It may be dramatic, hopeless, and "terminally unique." The point of this chapter is to offer some other possible vistas that may help to frame dynamics more in the realm of what is normal, expectable, and imminently resolvable.

As you will repeatedly see throughout this book, the nature of the journey of relationships is to move through varied stages. At many junctures, the feelings or circumstances of the two partners seem or even are diametrically opposed, locked in what appears to be a paralytic impasse. Demoralized, the two think, "We're incompatible! We're finished! Irreconcilable differences. There is no way out of this ... " This is the very stuff of couples work throughout the lifespan. Yes, repeatedly we hit those snares where it appears our interests are hopelessly at odds. The trauma and neglect family is usually a closed system, a zero-sum game. If one gets, the others don't, and there is no experience of repair. This book is all about healing those missing experiences, finding those missing pieces.

The purpose of Part I was to lay out the basics of relationship. Most of us missed the Relationship 101 course and so do not necessarily know how ordinary some of our difficulties might be, how very within the realm even of the mundane they are. The travails of trauma and neglect are layered upon a foundation that may be less pathological than you had imagined. These are the layers that virtually everyone must deal with. Teasing apart the elements may make the larger task more manageable.

The journey begins with a good assessment of where we are, a sorting through of the data. What do you see about your attachment styles? Can you identify yours and your partner's?

How able are you to see through your partner's eyes? How much do you know each other's worlds? Can you understand and respect your partner's point of view, however different, weird, or even offensive it might seem? Remembering you don't have to agree, can you validate it? Can you be empathic with each other?

How is your communication? Are there areas that need work in that arena?

How is your positive-to-negative ratio? Are you sufficiently generous to keep the relationship afloat?

And are there differences that you might chalk up to gender and not some fatal flaw in your partner or yourself? These are the questions posed to you by Part I.

And what, you might ask does any of this have to do with sex?

"Everything!" I say.

Part II

# A SHORT COURSE ON TRAUMA AND NEGLECT

Chapter Six

# IT'S THE END OF THE WORLD AS WE KNOW IT: A PRIMER ON TRAUMA

Before winnowing out the gross and subtle distinctions between childhood trauma and neglect, I must make two essential points. First, neglect is unquestionably a category of trauma in its own right. Neglect *is* a form of trauma.

And secondly, the two experiences are largely interwoven. Most if not all survivors of trauma and neglect have *both* trauma and neglect. Bad things happen to children who are not being taken care of; and generally it is parents who are absent or inattentive who tolerate or fail to see that their children are being abused or harmed. I take as given that most children of neglect and trauma suffered both. Generally, however, for any given individual, one or the other experience is dominant or primary.

This chapter will shine a light on overt trauma, also referred to as "shock trauma" or "incident trauma," viewing it from four different vantage points. We will examine trauma's impact on physiology, emotional life, cognition (the thinking mind), and relationship. Of course, these categories are integrally related, yet each has its own story to tell. Traumatic experience has left its powerful stamp on each of them in unique ways.

And what exactly is trauma? By definition, trauma is *overwhelming* experience. It is a stimulus that is greater than what the organism was designed to withstand and process by its usual means. Under these circumstances, the instinctual drive for survival impels extraordinary or "unusual" measures or adaptations to find a way to stay alive. By its very definition, the traumatic experience or event is in some way beyond the pale, so the response to it is of necessity an aberration from the norm. To respond in a normative manner would not suffice in a situation that is too extreme. The organism *must* resort to extreme measures. Do some of your partner's reactions, responses, and behaviors (or your own) seem "over the top," disproportional, crazy, or not "normal"? We shall see why.

## A BIT OF HISTORY

The science and study of trauma is relatively new. Only since 1980 have we even had the diagnostic label of Post-Traumatic Stress Disorder, which was impelled by the return of surviving troops from the war in Vietnam. After witnessing and being embroiled in protracted horror, the young soldiers came home to a political climate that by the war's end was the opposite of a hero's welcome. The general public attitude of disdain, regret, and waste about that war was the icing on their traumatic cake. The numerous and glaring problems of these vets ultimately garnered much-needed attention. Prior to this war, symptomatic "shell-shocked" war veterans were harshly judged as cowardly or weak and for the most part blamed rather than helped.

And what was this dramatic symptom picture? Vietnam vets were haunted by unrelenting nightmares; intrusive thoughts about their Vietnam experiences interfered with their attempts to build new postwar lives. They were visited by flashbacks, dramatic moments of recall in which, beyond remembering, they relived horrific moments from the war as if they were happening now. They suffered from depression and numbness and so avoided potentially stressful situations. They were disabled by paralyzing anxiety and fear. Many resorted to persistent substance abuse and addictions in desperate attempts to wash out the agony of their other symptoms, which of course served ultimately to compound them. Relationship may have been their worst agony of all.

With the advent of the women's movement at around the same historical time period, violence against women and children became a focus of concern and outrage. Researchers studying the constellation of symptoms of these seemingly diverse populations began to formulate an interesting and remarkably consistent diagnostic picture. War veterans, battered women, abused children, and victims of rape appeared to have much in common, and psychological trauma emerged as a subfield.

Knowledge about trauma surged dramatically forward in the 1990s, which came coincidentally to be referred to as the Decade of the Brain. Neuroimaging technologies made it possible to observe and photograph the living brain in action, and scientists now had a window into the precise impact of trauma on the nervous system. If it seems as if trauma alters the entire world as we know it, it is because it really does.

Relationship is about understanding your partner's world. Have you ever wondered why your trauma survivor partner does not just "cut it out"? This section will attempt to make sense of those times when something that does not seem like a big deal to you seems to leave your partner fearing for life and limb or somehow unleashes World War III between you.

## SCARED OUT OF MY MIND: SPEECHLESS TERROR

In 1996, Bessel van der Kolk, the veritable father of the young trauma subfield, together with a team of colleagues, published a most remarkable study. They recruited a group of heroic trauma survivor research subjects who allowed them to induce full-blown trauma flashbacks, and while in the state of high trauma activation, they submitted to having their brains scanned. The pictures are indeed worth many thousands of words, and for nearly 15 years they have been hanging framed on my office wall. I use them to illustrate what my traumatized clients observe in themselves or their partners, often on an anguished regular basis.

In the moment of trauma, the instantaneous experience of the individual is "I am going to die!" It is not necessarily a conscious thought; most likely it is not. The organism just knows this is a dire emergency. Self-preservation trumps all our impulses, so the body economizes and goes instantaneously into survival mode, reserving all its resources for this emergency. It is like running from a tiger: There is simply nothing else to do, nothing else that matters, just run! All functions, therefore, not absolutely necessary, such as digestion, ovulation, or abstract or distracting thought, just turn off. Blood flows away from the extremities and into the large muscles required for running or self-defense.

And what do we see in the brain scan? This is what is most illuminating for our purposes. First we look at the left hemisphere of the brain. The left prefrontal cortex in the front of the brain is the thinking mind, responsible for logical and analytical reason. This is the part of the brain that knows "I am an adult now, living in the 21st century." This is the part of the brain that knows "This is my partner who loves me, not an enemy poised to harm me."

Also in the left hemisphere of the brain are the speech centers. Speech comprehension resides in Wernicke's area and speech expression in Broca's area, both in the left temporal lobe. In the brain scan photos, the entire left hemisphere is dark, which means there is no activity going on, no neurons firing. Indeed, much of the brain is dark. One brain area, however, is lit up like a Christmas tree: the limbic area in the right hemisphere, home of the emotions and most notably the fight/flight response.

What does this mean? It means that in the moment of trauma (or of traumatic re-experiencing as in the case of our research subjects), the brain goes into a state where one *cannot think or speak*. In effect, the only brain areas that are online and the only available functions are to run, fight, or freeze. In short, the traumatic event overwhelms the organism, tripping the immediate reaction of mortal fear, and then the rapid activation of the survival mechanism. Nothing else matters.

Have you ever been stunned and baffled, let alone hurt or terrorized by your partner's sudden and intense reaction to a seemingly benign (to you) interaction? After a romantic and sweetly intimate date early in their relationship, Lois and Steve attempted to make love for the first time. Within a few moments of erotic touch, Lois was seized by a full-scale panic attack. Steve reacted first with shock and guilt, "What have I done?" Then came a rapid flow of shame, confusion, frustration, sadness, fear, rejection, even anger, and the strongest impulse to get away as fast and as far as possible.

Have you ever been shocked and incredulous when your partner did not seem even to remember the interaction or the stinging words? What *was* that all about?

## TRIGGERING AND REACTIVITY

One of the key structures of the limbic system is the amygdala, the fear center of the brain. Once overwhelmed by trauma, the amygdala becomes acutely sensitized. Hell-bent on never going through *that* again, it becomes hyperprotective and vigilant for any historical relic in the environment. It is on high alert for any potential threat. A sight, sound, or smell even vaguely reminiscent of the trauma can activate the amygdala and the thought "Oh no! It's happening again!" So can a familiar taste, a song, or a touch on a particular body part. To a Vietnam veteran, a random helicopter passing overhead can rudely awaken the memory, and although it is 40 years later and there is currently no real danger, the body might react as if the horrors of war were happening all over again now. Similarly, your loving and well-intentioned wet kiss or whisper of endearment can unleash a tirade, a blow, or a complete shutdown. And you can think, "I didn't *do* anything! Why are you treating me this way?"

We spoke previously about "stepping on your partner's sore toe." It is easy to activate your partner's trauma, wittingly or unwittingly saying or doing something that powerfully ignites traumatic memory. You are not a perpetrator but a stimulus. What you are doing or saying is not intrinsically "wrong" or "bad," nor was the passing helicopter that happened by. This is precisely what makes an explosive mine field of life in relationship for a traumatized person. Is it any wonder that many survivors of trauma isolate themselves for years and some even for whole lifetimes? This is what can be so wearing on those attempting to love them. Is it any wonder that partners throw up their hands and exclaim, "There is nothing I can do"? We shall return to these confounding dynamics at length.

Before we move on from this brief and perhaps discouraging section about physiology, I must add that the nascent study of trauma has seeded and cultivated a hotbed of inspired creativity and innovation in pursuit of ways out of the purgatory perpetrated by trauma. Powerful methodologies have emerged that can weaken and eventually extinguish the flammable traumatic spark, processing the memories so they can take their rightful place in the past. That creative trend continues to this day.

Happily, the Decade of the Brain uncovered a previously unknown and hopeful fact: the brain is "plastic" through the lifespan. Where previously we believed that neurons die as we move through life and do not regenerate, we now know that *neurogenesis*, or the production of new neurons, can continue as we continue living. Understanding the impact of trauma on the brain therefore is *not* a life sentence of doom. Healing is imminently possible in all its dimensions as the brain heals and grows.

Finally, the attachment researchers discovered another reason for optimism and another powerful incentive to process trauma: The surest predictor of secure attachment is when parents are able to make sense out of their own histories. Parents who know and can tell their own coherent autobiographical stories, with the left prefrontal brain regions all online, are the ones who can provide the foundation for a secure attachment for their own children, thereby breaking the chain. For those who have or wish to have children of their own, this may be an ultimate reason to hang in there with the difficult work of recovery.

## IT'S MORE THAN A FEELING

Have you ever stayed in a hotel near a freeway or airport? The incessant din of rushing cars or rumbling planes is like ambient air. The background roar is a chronic fact of life of the environment. At times the noise is an unbearable, crazy-making irritant; at other times it can vanish from awareness, being such a customary backdrop to everything; sometimes it can make an essential activity like sleep or concentration on a task impossible. Where some people might successfully ignore it, others simply can't escape it. Such is the interminable hum of fear in the nervous system of a traumatized person. It may be blanketed by weighty depression or masquerade as anger or control, but in reality what rules the traumatized person's life is one or another variation of terror. Trauma instates a hierarchy with fear at its pinnacle, a turbocharged engine that runs on fear. Fear is intimately tied to the brain physiology we have been looking at as well as to the body reactions of flooding stress hormones, racing heart, shallow breath, and tense muscles.

Fear, whether or not one is aware of it as such, powerfully shapes behavior. Matt's meanness was often shocking. Even his jokes were offensive, confusing, or even cruel. Not only was he insulting to his partner, but in our couples sessions, he routinely took swipes at me. His childhood had been one of chronic violence and humiliation. He never knew when and from where the next blow would explode. Beset with vigilant terror, Matt developed a personality much like a moat with alligators. His interface with the world and with his wife was the gnashing of daunting alligator teeth. Who would imagine that underneath all that bravado and intimidation huddled a little boy wracked with insecurity and terror, only wishing for protection and love? Who would feel the compassion and kindness he longed for? The love and care he craved were readily extinguished by his aggression.

Celia, because she was so afraid of being taken unawares again, strove for airtight predictability in her life, planning, structuring, and controlling everything she could. She did not think of it as fear. She just preferred having things done "right." Her partner and friends found her orderliness, repetitiveness, and inflexibility to be tyrannical and stifling. There was no room for anything or anyone else, no chance for a glimmer of spontaneity, variety, or impromptu aliveness. What her partner thought of as novelty, exploration, or fun made her feel nervous and unsafe. It seemed to the outside world as if she were just rigid and selfish, which of course deeply pained her and made her feel like a pariah whom nobody liked.

Dan's adaptation was to avoid and isolate. As long as he confined himself to his high-level tech job and steered clear of other people, he was successful and appeared not to suffer. Who would guess how much he was ruled by his fear? People thought he was a brilliant, aloof absent-minded professor off in his own world.

There are countless character adaptations to a nervous system and body dominated by fear. Character is precisely that: some sort of survival-based strategy for managing or coexisting with the fear.

Often the adaptations of character, initially designed to assist with coping, create a whole new set of problems and even dangers. It may help us find our way to compassion for either ourselves or our partners if we begin to understand the annoying, insulting, incomprehensible, or unbearably painful character adaptations we see or live with as ways to cope with fear. This is not to say we agree to *like* these behaviors or choose to keep living with them, but rather we make sense out of them. The sooner we stop reacting against them, in ourselves or our partners, the better our chances at taming, calming, and altering them. More about this later!

The amygdala is the seat of all the emotions, not only fear. Fear does rule the roost; there are other emotions on board as well. We have noted depression and sadness as being part of the trauma picture. Another powerful player is shame, and sometimes a weighty self-pity. What is your predominant emotional tone? What is your primary strategy for managing fear? What do you think is its impact on the people around you? How is it working for you?

## THAT'S MY STORY AND I'M STICKING TO IT

Cognition refers to the thinking mind, including such processes as aware-ness, perception, reasoning, and judgment. Trauma affects cognition in two predominant ways. The first, as we encountered in the brain scans, is that trauma can extinguish the thinking brain areas during the actual events or during flashback episodes of recall. Unable to think in those moments, memory may be logged in a fragmented, discontinuous, or chaotic way, if at all. Cognition can also be dulled when trauma activation is less extreme. Jude, for the first months of our couples sessions, had a very difficult time staying "present," meaning attentively and actively tracking or participating in the conversations. The content was close enough to her trauma to, if not turn off the prefrontal cortex completely, certainly dim it. When her partner attempted to process a difficult interaction they'd had during the week, often she struggled to even remember it, which of course frustrated him even further. The more we worked, the more present she became, but at first her partner felt utterly hopeless and abandoned by how "zoned out" or "not there" she was.

The other powerful way that trauma affects thinking is the way it becomes the lens through which the world is viewed. Everyday experience is perceived and interpreted through the filter of the trauma. A helicopter is not just a helicopter. A kiss is not just a kiss. Life is infused with meanings that hearken back to the trauma. A soldier whose entire battalion of buddies was blown away before his eyes may conclude, "You shouldn't get close to anyone because they just die." A person who was used and abused for sex might believe, "Sex is about being an object of someone else's horny whim and pleas-ure. No one will care how I feel. There is nothing in it for me." Cognitions and whole belief systems are shaped by the traumatic experience. Like a one-trick pony, the trauma story becomes the template for every subsequent story, regardless of your or my best intentions.

Again, and I will keep emphasizing this, healing is imminently possible! And relationship work is one of the most powerful ways to effect healing.

## "HELL IS OTHER PEOPLE"

Perhaps the gravest casualty of trauma is in the area of relationship. Despair, loneliness, and frustration in relationships are probably the primary motivators for traumatized people to seek help. The human animal is designed to be in relationship, and when we chronically fail at relationships, life becomes a kind of living hell.

Because the experience of trauma primes the brain and body to anticipate danger, anything that cannot be predicted or controlled is inherently risky. Relationships and other people can hardly be predictable or controllable, so what we most crave becomes a potential source of great harm. In effect, the "dilemma without solution" of the disorganized/disoriented attachment style is replicated across the board in the traumatized person's world: The source of danger and the object of longing are one and the same. So the traumatized person is ever in the disequilibrium of reaching toward and pulling back from that other. Sound familiar?

*Safety* is a key word in the trauma survivor's lexicon. Many partners get deathly tired of hearing the words "I don't feel safe . . . " If the trauma was interpersonal, that is if it was perpetrated by a person (as opposed to an earthquake or an animal), the key player in the original trauma story becomes the redundant character in whose image we are all created, whether or not we bear any true resemblance to that person at all. It is of course an agony for all involved. And because sexuality requires a fair measure of safety and physical calm (for all species), it will often be a particularly charged aspect of relationship life.

Another puzzling and insidious way that trauma can invade relationship life is what is referred to as the Stockholm Syndrome, a term coined by a Swedish criminologist following a famous bank robbery in 1973, when he observed how hostages became attached to their brutal captors and even defended them. In a similarly baffling way, traumatized people might unwittingly be attracted to people who resemble or behave like the perpetrators of their trauma. In effect, they realize their worst fear: It does happen again.

Because of the prefrontal shutdown during trauma, memory may reside in the brain in a wordless, pictureless, cognitionless way. And being a story that needs to be told, it might express itself in the form of re-enactment. Much as a traumatized child might endlessly recreate the frightening episode in repetitive play, a traumatized adult may unwittingly recreate the scene in current life by choosing to relate to people who behave like the characters from childhood. Even if the partner does not necessarily resemble the perpetrator, still somehow the trauma story can unconsciously choreograph and display itself between them.

Rosemary had a terrible history of emotional abuse, rejection, and abandonment. She had felt hated by her whole family. Her partner Lou made an effort to be patient, compassionate, empathic, and accepting. Rosemary, true to her trauma story, constantly felt rejected and abandoned by Lou. She heard Lou's words completely differently from how they were intended or remembered them in a distorted and insulting way. Bereft, she would persistently accuse her partner of not liking her and wanting to get rid of her or of cheating. Lou worked hard to stay kind and forgiving, but after a while the unending complaints would reach a tipping point and Rosemary's worst fear would come true. It is the nature of trauma to re-enact the trauma.

## SUMMING UP

Admittedly, this introduction to trauma is a lot to digest. We looked at how the experience overwhelms every aspect of a person's being. Our reason for laying out this much detail is not to level blame, certainly not to locate a "problem child" or "identified patient." We have obviously just begun with one half of the couple.

Many partners balk at my adamant belief that all relationship is a 50–50 proposition wherein both partners contribute equally to the difficulty, just in different ways. That's *my* story and I'm sticking to it! I also emphasize yet again, as bleak as the trauma picture might appear, healing is imminently possible. I am so gratified that in the almost three decades that I have been involved with this work, new science and new methodologies continue to improve the possibilities of getting to a life of calm, joy, love, and even sex more and more effectively. Keep the faith!

For now, consider whether this chapter shed light on anything that makes sense of something about you and your partner. How might you make use of it?

# Chapter Seven

# WAITING FOR THE SUN TO COME OUT: WAKING UP TO NEGLECT

Ian was offended and annoyed when I proposed that he was a child of neglect. "My dad died when I was five and my little brother was three. My mom worked really hard to take care of us. I think she did a pretty darn good job." He loved his mother, a kind woman who had been through a lot. He felt as if I were insulting and slandering her. And Ian also was quite comfortable with the idea that it was his partner who had the rough childhood and needed to heal and change. Although he suffered from depression, anxiety, and aggression and could not seem to get things done, he just did not buy it that he had a trauma history of his own.

## INVISIBLE TRAUMA

In the early years of the twenty-first century, it became clear to a team of leaders in the field of psychological trauma that a whole category of traumatized children was slipping through the cracks. The diagnosis of Post-Traumatic Stress Disorder initially designed to catalog symptoms and create treatment methods for war veterans, brought public awareness and sympathy for the traumatized a long way. Yet over time it became apparent that the experiences of trauma of adult (if one can think of 18- to 20-year-olds as adults) soldiers, of battered or sexually assaulted women, and of young abused children were in significant ways quite different. Some of the symptoms on the official diagnostic checklist did not fit for traumatized children, and some of the special problems of children did not show up on the list. Too many suffering children, not quite diagnosable as the codes are written, were floating under the radar without getting the help they needed.

There is an odd chicken-and-egg relationship between diagnosis and culture. As we saw with the PTSD diagnosis, an official medical name and treatment programs to go with it change public attitude and medical and political policy. These changes validate and lend respect and credibility to the traumatized and their experience, which in turn affects public opinion and policy, and history proceeds from there. This change has not yet happened around the invisible trauma of neglect, which may be even more prevalent and more damaging than its overt trauma counterpart. Such a change in thinking certainly had not reached people like Ian.

Overt or incident trauma is about what *did* happen; neglect is about what *did not* happen. Many adult children of neglect will accurately declare, "But nothing happened to me!" "Exactly!" I say. Many, many things are *supposed* to happen, and the composite of these missing experiences is the grievous injury. We now know that attachment to caregivers, especially early in life, is foundational for brain and character development. A child left too much on his or her own resources suffers in many ways. In the words of one adult child of neglect, "I was not known, had nowhere to go, and nothing to do." Of course, as with all other experiences and all other organisms, they find ways to adapt.

Because our culture forged of rugged individualism admires and even idealizes self-reliance, we may not even notice the liability of a child being perhaps too independent or too much the caretaker of self and others. So this population has been additionally neglected by both culture and psychotherapy. Thankfully, that is slowly beginning to change. The scars of neglect, however, are most visible in the realm of relationship, at least to those who are paying attention.

## WHAT IS NEGLECT?

By definition, neglect is the failure to provide for essential needs of a child, be they physical, emotional, or educational. Such failure can of course include failure to provide safety, supervision, or guidance or failure to protect the child from witnessing violent or traumatic scenes between parents or other family members. What I see most often in my office are adult children of emotional neglect whose caregivers were depressed, substance abusing, or traumatized themselves and thus unable or ineffectual at being a reliable presence. Others, however, like Ian's mother, may have been just plain busy. Burdened with single parenthood, too many children, a troubled marriage, illness, or poverty, they may have been preoccupied or somehow ill-equipped to attend to this child. So indeed the child experiences not being known, and minimal "mirroring" of his or her feeling world.

Children learn who they are and what they feel through seeing it in a caregiver's eyes. The ritualized cooing conversations between infants and parents are a kind of musical dialog between them, where the adult is reflecting back to the child, "I see you, how happy I am to see you!" Or it may be "Oh, you are scared now, it is OK, it's going to be OK . . . " A flow of emotion rallies back and forth between them. This flow is an important ingredient in the brain's developing structures and circuits, in the child learning about emotions and eventually the names of emotions, and even the sense of existence as a being. These seemingly trivial interactions are in fact essential developmental inputs.

My portrait of the child of neglect has its roots in the attachment theory depiction of the avoidantly attached. This is the infant with the absent or dismissive mother. The picture, however, is heavily marbled with my observation over two decades of dozens of men and women who shared key traits that shaped themselves into a distinct profile, which although not scientifically researched has served as a consistent and useful model.

I recently heard a colleague tell the story about his beloved golden retriever named Streak. Streak was an old dog, almost 15 years old, which is getting up there for a retriever. One day Streak, excited and delighted to see his owner arrive home, leapt out the door at lightning speed and dashed out into the street. To the horror of my colleague, in the space of an instant Streak was beneath the wheels of an oncoming car. My colleague flew to his rescue and when he could not coax Streak to move, reached his hands rather forcefully under Streak's bleeding backside. Said my colleague, "Then Streak did something he had never done before. He bit me . . . He did not bite me because he was angry. He bit me because he was in pain." Something about this story reminded me of countless neglect survivors I have known who seem to have a well of quiet (or not so quiet) aggression. It is often buried or outside of awareness, and is really an expression of deep and lonely pain.

## WAITING FOR THE SUN

Probably my greatest, certainly my most beloved teacher about neglect is my husband Michael. Early in our relationship when we found ourselves yet again stymied by a tangle of triggering and disconnection, he would shrug, roll his eyes, throw up his hands, and exasperatedly say to me, "I'll just sit here and wait for the sun to come out." I was of course instantly enraged, even more uncontrollably upset than before. The implication was that the conflict was all *my* fault and that as soon as I just calmed down or got myself together, the weather would clear and all would be well between us. It was all up to me. I was furious because as ever, responsibility for the trouble and for its solution was all on me.

What I later learned is that Michael's history of neglect taught him to truly believe that. The experience of neglect is that in relationship, the child has no impact. That child is in fact powerless over whether attention rains or shines or vanishes entirely. It was completely arbitrary. Michael's childhood taught him, "There's nothing you can do, so just wait."

The signature of neglect is passivity. The clarion cry or moan of the child of neglect is, "I don't know what to do," or "There's nothing I can do." In that first partners' workshop, I was amazed that although all the men were brilliantly smart and successful in all kinds of ways, just like Michael, in relationship they felt, and in effect were, utterly helpless and clueless. What a remarkable, perhaps unbelievable irony alongside exquisite competence, resourcefulness, and independence.

## I CAN'T LIVE WITH OR WITHOUT YOU

In the early days of attachment theory, Mary Ainsworth, a colleague of John Bowlby's, designed a research procedure to study infant attachment called the Strange Situation. It was a brief sequence, captured on now famous grainy black-and-white cellulose, in which infants were observed in distinct stages of separation and reunion. In the first scene, the infant is playing with the mother in a small playroom, and after a short while the mother departs. In the second scene a friendly woman, unfamiliar to the child, enters the room, interacts briefly with the child, and then exits. Shortly thereafter, the mother returns. The whole series is but a few minutes, and at each transition the child's emotional, behavioral, and physiological reactions are carefully monitored.

In the classic films, the avoidant infant is playing with blocks quietly in the corner by himself. He looks serious and self-contained, even contented. He is not interested in having his mother play with him. When she leaves the room, he appears nonchalant, as if he does not register her absence. The arrival of the stranger does not capture his attention, nor does her attempt to join him in play. When she leaves, he is unfazed. The mother returns and the child continues to appear as if he just can't be bothered. Only his physiology gives him away. His little body registers all the markers of high anxiety in heart rate, skin conductance, and stress hormones. Cool as a cucumber on the outside, this little person is profoundly affected by the comings and goings of important others but has submerged feelings so deeply that before long he cannot even feel them himself. Neglect teaches this infant early on that it is pointless to protest or even cry. He learns to conserve energy, to block out the importance of attachment, to do for himself. "If I don't need anyone, I won't be disappointed or hurt. I'll never get what I need from another person anyway. The only trouble comes with need. If I am self-sufficient, I am fine." All of this begins long before he is a year old, long before he has cognition or language. And in our culture, especially little boys are praised for this and viewed as very good. Remind you of anyone you know?

## NO THERE THERE

Receiving so little attention, the child of neglect has a decidedly external focus. It is through the experience of someone else taking an interest in his or her feelings that a child discovers and becomes curious about them. When that does not happen, awareness of feelings might not happen either. Needs are eliminated, feelings don't emerge. It may even be hard for these kids to discern what they like or want. Inner life may be flat or empty for them. They may feel confused, guilty, or ashamed about being anxious or depressed, with nothing to point to as a cause. Exactly: nothing.

Again, the attachment literature describes the adult avoidant as having little memory of childhood or little childhood memory that involves other people. My experience with adult survivors of neglect is that they have vague or minimal awareness of their own story. They will be expert on the story of their partners and very focused and aware of their partners' traumatic difficulties. They may even have finely tuned memory regarding the details of their partners' progress through life, but in the words of Gertrude Stein, there is no there there. It is as if their experience taught them "There is no you."

For me initially, Michael's rapt attention was dazzling. It made me feel special, fascinating, important. But over time, it came to feel "rabid," intrusive, and abandoning. I wanted to feel as if there were someone *with* me, someone whom I could push against. Someone strong enough to protect me, and whom I did not have to worry could collapse or be destroyed by me!

## TOUCH

Attachment research revealed another tragic bit of data. Often the mother in the avoidant–dismissive dyad, to use the formal language, was repelled by the infant's body. She did not want to touch her child. One of the great deficits of neglect, and of all forms of trauma, is that the child misses out on the precious primal experience of being touched and held. And where the self-reliant character can resolve and surmount the challenges of most human needs, the need to be touched and held and ultimately for sex is harder to reconcile. One *can* provide it for oneself in some ways, but it is not the same. This conundrum, this one failure in the otherwise airtight strategy around need, creates a gnawing complication to which we will of course return.

Summing up, the experience of neglect leaves a gaping emotional void for an inner world. It is pointless to protest or cry, so need is sealed off and buried deep. This happens so early that the pain of it is as if tucked away in the coffin with the disavowed need. All is out of sight and mind. The child looks self-sufficient and autonomous and may even be proudly successful in the world of achievement. But in the interpersonal world, he or she feels powerless, impotent, mistrustful, and even scared. These children and then adults feel that they "can't." Because it is pointless to try, they don't.

In closing, childhood incident trauma and the trauma of childhood neglect have a crucially important key similarity that also bears powerfully on our endeavor. In both cases there is a glaring absence of repair. Repair is when a rupture, insult, hurt, or some other disconnection is followed by some sort of healing. It is when the adult takes the lead in facilitating a coming back into connection. It might be an apology, it might include a life lesson, it might be assistance or forgiveness or a comforting hug. It is a rescue from the roaring and deathlike shipwreck of loss that disconnection wreaks upon a child and later an adult. Without the repair, life's inevitable misattunements, misunderstandings, and missteps appear permanent, fatal, and terrifying, which makes the prospect of intimacy something akin to a suicidal pole vault.

## PRACTICE

The Strange Situation taught us that powerful indicators of attachment are embedded in our feelings and behaviors during separation and reunion. What do you notice about your behavior, emotions, and body experience around separation and reunion with your partner?

The four main junctures of separation and reunion during the day are waking, when the first partner leaves the home, when the last partner returns home from the day apart, and dropping off to sleep. These are vulnerable transitions from an attachment standpoint.

Here is a practice I learned from couples therapist extraordinaire Pat Love. At each of these four transitions points, insert a positive attachment ritual of about 30 to 60 seconds: a hug, a compliment, an appreciation, or some unique ritual of your own creation. At these four times of day, implement that brief activity. Try it for a week and see what you notice!

Chapter Eight

# DO YOU WANNA DANCE? MORE ABOUT TRIGGERING AND ADAPTATION

The word "triggering" gets tossed around a lot and has a rather harsh and violent ring to it, conjuring perhaps guns and cowboys' horses. What does it really mean? A "trigger" is generally *not* a weapon or a hostile act per se. Often in and of itself it may be quite innocuous. A trigger is a stimulus or catalyst, like the veteran's helicopter. It works as a "protective" reminder, activating traumatic recall, often stealthily and at lightning speed. And because trauma elicits a quick and decisive survival-based reaction, activated memory is likely to do the same.

As we described earlier, the brain of a traumatized person becomes highly sensitized to cues reminiscent of past dangers. The entire organism, poised for prevention of more pain and loss, is constantly scanning. When it perceives potential threat, it defaults to behaviors of fight, flight, or freeze, which might appear to make no sense at all in present time or certainly seem disproportional to the stimulus in the eyes of an observer.

Much of what we remember, certainly from early in our lives, is remembered wordlessly. It might be a feeling or sensation that when we re-experience it, we are not even aware that we are remembering something. It may just be discomfort or emotion that stirs a response. It may all *seem* to be about now. That is why the world of triggering and reactivity is so insidious. Layers of experience, much of it intense, are all mixed up together, and it can be difficult to tease apart what is "real." Often triggered reactions appear quite ridiculous or even "crazy."

Celia's story about the porch light later became an embarrassment to her. It is one clear illustration. As a child she felt invisible and imagined she did not matter to anyone at all. She felt as if no one knew or cared about her comings and goings or even her existence. Early in her marriage, she developed a hair trigger about the porch light. When she came home after a long day at work and the doorway was dark, her reaction was instantaneous and extreme. She was pitched into a pit of violent old feelings: She felt unwelcome, forgotten, unwanted, invisible, unimportant, and all this before she even set foot in the house! No matter if 14 out of 15 times the light was on, no matter if it was a malfunctioning porch light timer, she fumed with hurt and rage, and the evening was of course shot.

In childhood, Celia had adapted to feeling invisible and insignificant with a swift and silent withdrawal. "That was how I made myself safe," she declared. "If I'm invisible, I'm fine! I'll just retreat to my own private world and forget all of you! I did just that." As an adult, when triggered by the porch light, she defaulted to the old adaptation, which of course had a deadly impact on her partner Lou.

Although being unwelcome or forgotten may seem a far cry from a threat to life, in the world of attachment trauma, such experiences can *feel* like dying to a child. (In Celia's case, sometimes being invisible and unprotected made her vulnerable to other untoward experiences.) The point is that Lou did not do anything terrible. Perhaps Lou "stepped on her sore toe." But Celia's reaction was as if he were thoughtless, uncaring, and mean. All of his sterling qualities and loving behavior were completely forgotten in those moments. She was righteously incensed, and each time it happened again served as "evidence."

Of course there is another side to this story. Lou, being a child of neglect, had a mother who was absent both literally and figuratively, which felt deathly to the little guy. Celia's long days were a trigger for him. Much like the avoidant toddler in the Strange Situation experiment, his adaptation was to be self-sufficient and self-contained and to busy himself with his own activity. He did in fact train himself to forget about her. So when Celia felt forgotten, she was in fact partly right. But not for the reasons she thought!

## COULDN'T YOU JUST . . .

Much as Celia would have liked to believe that the solution to the recurring porch light havoc was for Lou to just turn on the porch light, that is not the answer. This is a hard sell, but I am committed to it. We are *each responsible for our own triggering*. It was *Celia's* work to process her childhood feelings of being invisible and unimportant so she would not be so readily flammable by an innocent mistake. Similarly, Lou would have liked to believe that if she just changed her schedule and came home earlier, the recurring nightmare would be eliminated. It was in fact *his* work to process his childhood feelings about being marginal or abandoned. When they each did that, the porch light drama stopped.

Granted, it is in each of our best interests to learn where the land mines are and avoid triggering our partners. It makes life easier and more pleasant *for me* when my partner is not triggered and vice versa. It is a good goal; however, it is not my responsibility, nor is it my partner's responsibility to tiptoe around and refrain from triggering me.

## "EARNED" ATTACHMENT STATUS

Besides enhancing peace and harmony, there is another good reason to process our own childhoods. In the early days of my work as a couples therapist, immersed in the theory and research about attachment, I learned of some fascinating work going on right here in my neck of the woods. The Strange Situation research experiment, after being replicated hundreds, perhaps thousands of times, had become the gold standard in assessing attachment styles of infants and children. Subsequent research showed that attachment styles formed in infancy tend to remain intact through the decades, indeed through the lifespan. This means that the child who had an initial avoidant pattern like the little boy we visited in the last chapter is likely to retain his relationship characteristics, continuing to be self-contained, independent, self-reliant, and perhaps aloof and anxious. The same is true for the characteristics of the other styles.

Some brilliant attachment psychologists in Berkeley made some additional groundbreaking discoveries. They learned that attachment patterns could be changed and reshaped later in life by intentionally working on them, which is certainly good news for us! Attachment theory helps us to understand why we and our partners react and relate as we do. It sheds light on missing experiences that we might be able to recreate in the present, thereby altering attachment status. The Berkeley researchers called this "earned" secure attachment. We need not be stuck indefinitely with our old patterns!

Interestingly, the key ingredient for earning secure attachment status in adulthood lies in what the Berkeley group called the "coherent narrative." Childhood experience, particularly traumatic experience, is logged in a fragmented way. As we saw, in moments of trauma, the left thinking and verbal hemisphere of the brain ceases to function. So what is stored in memory is often discontinuous and impressionistic. It does not hang together like a linear, flowing story. The many disjointed pieces, some sensory, some emotional, some bits of visual, some partial explanations of events, may not seem to make sense. Completing the often long and arduous task of processing and stringing together the many and dissonant beads of experience into a single continuous autobiographic strand and coming to understand, "Oh, this is what happened to me and this is how it affected me" is the key to "earned secure attachment." And that is how the intergenerational chain is broken, and we can provide a secure attachment to our own kids.

What do you know about your own hot buttons? What do you know about your partner's? How much have you sorted and made sense of your own story?

## Chapter Nine

# CYCLES OF ESCALATION: IT TAKES TWO TO TANGLE

*Systems that can be perturbed from outside and incorporate external influences in their future behavior possess a remarkable capacity for learning and growth even though they live within boundaries defined by simple rules. By adhering to these lower-level rules, something greater than the sum of its parts can emerge. The emergent level is thus quite different from the level it springs from. If the component relationships within the system become optimized for a particular task as a result of external perturbations, the system is called adaptive. The brain is such an adaptive complex system.*

As soon as I laid eyes on Jeremy and Shawna, the afternoon of their first appointment, I spotted it. Before either of them even spoke. They both had the look of a threadbare carpet, the worn, unfinished, scuffed floor showing through. They looked exhausted, pale, sad, confused, and uncertain. I guessed that they were in that nightmarish stage of relationship where they are in a chronic state of mutual triggering. As soon as they began to describe what brought them, it was clear that such was the case.

Jeremy was a rock star, both literally and figuratively. He was a professional musician, enjoying the sexiness of the hip, public eye. Having grown up in Israel where life had been rugged and harsh, he had a brassy, proud self-confidence that bordered on superiority. He was utterly convinced that it was Shawna who had serious problems.

Shawna, also very attractive, had the posture and a bearing of fear and caution. In spite of being intelligent and creative, she struggled with life and with the daily demands of making a living. She was tall and slender, but her crouched shoulders and downcast eyes made her look small, tentative, and childlike. At least partially, she bought into Jeremy's assessment of her. Another part of her was furious and insulted by it. Both partners were exasperated to the point of wondering if it were too late, or simply not worth it, to start couples therapy now. They had been teetering with indecision for a while: get married or go their separate ways? And Shawna's biological clock was ticking.

As they described it, they fought constantly, about "everything," but many of their fights were about sex. Jeremy railed about the poverty of sex in their relationship and Shawna's "guaranteed" rejection of his advances. Angry, critical, and sometimes even vengeful, he might muse out loud about other women or about leaving the relationship. He frequently made pointed remarks about how Shawna really needed to be "cured." Of course, Jeremy's anger, criticism, and haughty or demanding tone were anything but erotic or attractive to Shawna. Beyond being turned off, she was terrified. She would generally cower in the face of his anger and withdraw into defensiveness, feeling not understood, threatened, and unclear about his intentions.

Shawna's father was a public figure, handsome, charismatic, and successful outside the home. In private, he was moody, with often violent, unpredictable blasts of anger. Theirs was a trophy family, and Shawna felt like a pretty possession on display. Her mother had been self-absorbed and distracted, and when early on her father began sexually abusing Shawna, her mother looked the other way, much as she always had with his fits of temper. Shawna believed that she was in fact worthless. Her only value in the world was to be used as a showpiece or a recreational toy. Being an object or being brutalized or ignored by both parents made sense to her. And because there was lots of money, great clothes, and fancy schools, she was expected to feel privileged. Instead she felt guilty.

Jeremy thought Shawna *was* privileged compared to his stoic background. His family was of slim means, "salt of the earth"; both parents came from backgrounds of suffering and hard work. Jeremy himself had begun earning his own money however he could in his early teens. His culture admired self-reliance and he had come to the States alone as a youth to study. Although he missed his family, he was proud of how well he had done.

Jeremy's mother had worked outside the home since he was quite small. When his sisters were born, it was Jeremy who took care of the babies, and of necessity he had become a proficient cook before he was a teenager. Although unmarried, Jeremy and Shawna had been living together for 4 years when we met.

## WIMBLEDON REVISITED

It took no time at all to identify Jeremy and Shawna's tightly choreographed, repetitive pattern of conflict. It constellated around virtually any "issue" because the *apparent* issue was not *really* the issue. Jeremy assented to carry much more than half of the responsibility of their household. He made most of the money because Shawna was attempting to make a go of her own small business. He did much of the housework because he could not stand a mess and she seemed oblivious to the clutter. He cooked as he always had in his childhood home. He basically "asked nothing of her." So of course he felt entitled to at least "one small thing": a robust sex life—or at least a sex life at all.

Shawna wished for closeness. She did not care that much about the housework, even the specially prepared food. She wished for tenderness: that they might talk. She wished Jeremy would take an interest in her art like he had when they first met. She wished he would want to do things with her like hiking or going to plays or talking about what they were reading. He seemed only to value her for one thing, and beyond that he was perpetually angry, just like her angry father. She occupied herself with her work and her close women friends, but she was lonely.

The pattern could begin with either of them. Jeremy was "perpetually" angry, and his anger, reminiscent of her father's, was scary to Shawna. Her triggered reaction, much like her childhood reaction, was to avoid him as much as she could. Shawna's absence and unresponsiveness to his "meager" request triggered his childhood experience of being overly responsible and alone. Although ultra self-reliant, he was bitter about it, even demanding. Jeremy's increasing anger triggered Shawna's increasing withdrawal. Shawna's increasing withdrawal triggered intensified anger. The rapid-fire volley of triggering to reaction, with the reaction triggering a heightened reaction, which triggered a heightened reaction, triggering a still more heightened reaction ad infinitum, resembled all-star tennis. Whack, whack, whack, it was like Wimbledon with no winner.

I call these cycles of escalation because the trigger-to-reaction chicken-and-egg routine is circular and self-perpetuating, with each progressive loop building in momentum and intensity. I always worry when I see trauma and neglect couples in this stage. Repeatedly reactivating the brain circuitry of their worst traumatic experiences has an effect beyond retraumatizing both partners. It also spikes what is known as "the kindling effect": The more a given brain circuit is activated, the more vulnerable it becomes to getting activated again. Without help at this stage, traumatized couples can indeed make each other's trauma worse.

Another hazard of this stage is that each episode of traumatic triggering floods the body and brain with stress hormones. As stress hormones rush into available brain receptors, serotonin, the neurotransmitter of calm and well-being, is crowded out. The brain, bathed in stress hormones, defaults into serotonin debt, and because of the time lag for the serotonin to build back up again, plummets into a backlash of depression much like a hangover. Exhausted, depressed, and deep in the legacy of triggered childhood despair and hopelessness, both partners increasingly bear the haggard, telltale look I recognized when I first met Shawna and Jeremy.

## TIED TO THE WHIPPING POST

Adult children of trauma or neglect may or may not remember their silent, hidden screams or prayers of "Make it stop!" For most it never did stop, not until they got big enough to get away. Another triggered reaction to this stage, because they have no template for repair, is that this living hell will never end either. They fear that the only way to peace and safety is to leave. Why do they stay? And why do they straggle into my office? Often there truly is a core of real love between them. And I also believe that the psyche and the soul long for healing and deeply wish to discover a different outcome from the heartbreak they have known.

Because children are dependent and cannot leave, they must find a way to tolerate and survive their lonely and painful plight. Adults who survived were trained by their childhoods to endure and adapt somehow. When you ask, "Why do I stay?" with perhaps even shame and humiliation, it is precisely this childhood training that makes it possible, even makes sense of it. And there are also ways that childhood taught them to make it distinctly worse.

Shawna had no idea that to Jeremy, as a child of neglect, her withdrawal felt to Jeremy like the most heinous cruelty imaginable. Under all the bravado was a little boy who had suffered the desolate loneliness of preoccupied and absent parents and the despair of being too early and too much on his own. The brain develops in resonance, and with no one there as an anchor, mirror, and companion, the hollow, echoing solitude compromises it. While he convinced himself early that he was strong and tough and did not need anything, at his core he sadly grappled with a severe deficit of interpersonal learning and the belief that he would never get what he needed in relationship. Much as he almost boasted that it did not matter, in his heart of hearts, he knew that it did.

In her childhood home, silence, retreating into the safe haven of her room or staying late at school to work on art projects kept Shawna busy and safe. When she stayed away, avoided Jeremy, or just tuned him out, Shawna could imagine "I didn't *do* anything . . . I'm taking care of myself! He's just always angry." For Jeremy, her absences were a violent abandonment, like a dagger in his primal wound. Nothing incited his rage more bitterly or more instantly.

For Shawna, having her powerful father value her only for his sexual grati-fication repeatedly confirmed her deepest conviction "I don't matter at all." Jeremy's wish to have sex even when he was mad at her, or his entitled and self-centered attitude when they did have sex, added fuel to her simmering burn, not to mention the panic. Sometimes she resorted to a feminist argu-ment about objectification. Most of the time she just clammed up.

## THE RAT HOLE OF SELF-HATRED

One of Jeremy's frequent complaints was that Shawna was "selfish." (No matter that she thought the same about him.) Once sympathetic, he tired of her trauma stories, complaining that they were dramatic and self-indulgent. "Enough already, I know it was awful!" It was true that Shawna sometimes "explained" too much. Rather than listening to Jeremy's pain, she would "justify" her sexual difficulty or her fearful withdrawal, and he would once again feel that "Here we go again. It is all about you . . . "

But other times Shawna would default to an ancient childhood pattern I call the "rat hole of self-hatred." She would proceed to trash herself in Jeremy's presence. "You are right! I'm a worthless piece of excrement and you'd be much better off without me. Whatever I try to do makes things worse. I'm a blight on this planet and I would be better off dead. I should have killed myself as a kid like I always thought of doing. I was just too chicken to do it . . . " Yet these diatribes of self-condemnation were as angrily self-centered as her defensive explanations. They were equally disconnected from Jeremy's pain, so they did nothing to help him, nothing to facilitate reconnec-tion. Quite the opposite, they served to alienate and annoy Jeremy further, increasing the gaping distance.

## YEAH, YEAH, YEAH

Jeremy had a knee-jerk tendency to offer: He would offer to pay for things, he would offer to help Shawna with her business, he would take on more and more responsibility for the household and the dogs. Jeremy took pride in his generosity. The problem was the gnawing resentment that often followed his overoffering and overgiving. He frequently leapt to say yes without think-ing of what that yes might in fact mean to him. Could he really afford it, whether in money, time, or emotional stamina? Often not, but he realized it too late. He would find himself exhausted, short of time for his own priorities, in over his head, or broke. Then he would resent Shawna. Or he would believe he had somehow earned entitlement to something sexual or otherwise, even if the "deal" had been unspoken or just sealed inside his own head.

In childhood, helping had been an urgent attempt at being noticed in some way, or it was the only way to get anything he needed. Jeremy did not realize he was repeating something from his past with all of this "doing," and he also did not realize that he was rapidly losing Shawna's trust by supporting and then resenting her. "I don't feel safe to accept anything from you anymore. It feels like a trap or a trick, or an exchange of currency." It was painful that this sense of danger impelled her to push away the help she craved. The result was more rejection for Jeremy, more feelings of lonely worthlessness for Shawna.

## CYCLES OF ESCALATION: ANOTHER ONE BITES THE DUST

The good news about cycles of escalation is that both partners hold the possibility of achieving the lifelong fantasy of making it stop. The reason is simple: *It takes two to escalate.* Both Shawna and Jeremy worked hard to learn that if one of them triggered and the other did not react, the cycle did not ignite. Like a dud firework it fizzled, sputtered, and was quietly extinguished. If Jeremy made a biting comment about being sexually frustrated and Shawna stayed calm and nonreactive, Jeremy would eventually settle down and even feel remorse for his nastiness. This might even happen relatively quickly. He might still have the same feelings to express, but he would do so differently. Having the airspace clear of static and tension freed him to be more self-aware, which he increasingly came to be. Similarly, when Jeremy was able to manage his reaction to Shawna's withdrawal, she was less inclined to withdraw, or she did not withdraw as far or as long. Released from the immensely upsetting triggered reactions of the other, both began to make the unimaginable discovery of apology! Yes, Virginia, the ceasefire of cycles of escalation is imminently achievable by all. And how is this done?

## R. I. P.: LAYING THE TRAUMA STORY TO REST

There are three essential steps in interrupting the cycle of escalation. Again, this is anything but easy, but it is life-changing. In effect, this is the essence of trauma therapy in a nutshell. So do not expect of yourself that you will be able to quickly and independently achieve it. Since we are working with long-entrenched brain mechanisms originally wired in a survival-mode situation, they will be doggedly persistent and convincing. Go gently and with good help.

### Step One: Recognition

The first step may be the most important, because it is easy to be blinded by the trees and miss the forest. It can often seem as if the fight really is about the plans for the weekend; who should clean the bathroom; a birthday gift; or sex. Jeremy and Shawna could enact the same trigger–react sequence about any content. If the conversation tripped his "I'll never get what I need" or her "I don't matter" switch, they were off to the races. This can be encouraging, because it changes the focus from "We fight about absolutely everything" to "We have a handful of nagging and highly charged vulnerabilities." Big difference, in fact! As we become able to discern the live wires, the real conversation gradually becomes possible.

## Step Two: Identifying the Source

We have already covered the concept of the "big bang." So we know that whenever there is a big charge of emotion, some deep past injury has been bumped, nicked, or ripped back open. The challenge is having the humility and the patience to reflect and plumb the historical archives to unearth the template. I say humility and patience because when angry and hurt, we would all rather point an accusing finger at the other than rummage around in our own inner bone heaps; and when we are upset, real restraint is required to slow down and reflect. Period. If we can turn inward and locate the roots of the powerful reaction, we have the possibility of a new choreography and of altering the march of history.

The childhood material is not always obvious or transparent and sometimes defies language at first. Here is the story I told Jeremy and Shawna in response to their skeptical questions. Abraham had an explosive judgmental reaction when Lucy took "too long" to come to attend to their baby when she cried. He lambasted her with criticism, calling her self-centered, lacking in clear priorities, failing as a mother, and lacking in essential values. She was devastated and defensively lashed back with explanations for what she had to quickly do on her way to the baby. She insisted she was doing the best she could and he was simply clueless about what was required to be a mother.

Only when we stopped action and Abraham studied the feelings that erupted in him when their tiny, vulnerable baby cried and wailed did he recognize how familiar the howl of urgency and the comfort that did not come felt to *him*. There in our session, suddenly this large, burly Marlboro man looked different. His eyes darkened and had a glistening, sad faraway look. His chest ached and his limbs tensed as he crouched forward in the chair, seeming to hold himself. He did not have a picture or story memory of being a hungry infant waiting alone for an absent mother. But the sense of emergency and helplessness were deeply known to him, he could feel that. He knew that his mother had suffered postpartum depression and gone back to work when he was but 6 weeks old. So we could construct a comprehensible scenario for why his reaction was so extreme. This made sense to both him and Lucy and affected her much more than his reasoned criticism of her parenting. It also interrupted their cycle of escalation, amounting to a victory for all three of them.

### Step Three: Processing

It is through processing that the unintegrated fragments of traumatic experience are laid to rest. Rather than a potent newsreel of war poised to be repeatedly projected on the screen of live daily experience, they join the archives of past memory. A kiss becomes just a kiss, a helicopter becomes just a helicopter and no longer a startling alarm bell. The once-traumatic memory is logged as other nontraumatic autobiographical memory is logged, joining a continuous thread of consecutive life experience. It may still be accompanied by emotions. Certainly both Lucy and Abraham felt sadness for the lonely infant that had been evoked in Abraham's body. But the scene ceased to replay in present time.

How then is this feat accomplished? As we saw in the graphic display of the brain scan, essential parts of the trauma experience are lost to cognition and verbalization. Accessing the pieces we do have—the visual, the body sensation, and the emotion—and available details of the story, bringing those partial elements together into a rich braid, a semblance of a story line begins to form, and it makes sense. Granted, Abraham did not know from explicit recall that he was a neglected infant, so we want to be careful not to author an authoritative set of "facts." But the emotions that emerged in this big, strong guy as we discussed this scenario were profound and tender. And following these discussions, his reaction to Lucy and to their infant's cries was gradually changed. He still wanted her to be more organized and get to feeding the baby, but it no longer felt like a dire and life-threatening emergency.

The present time challenges of daily life do not simply disappear. As Jeremy and Shawna were quick to discover, once the cycle of reactivity resolved, they were in a position to craft a sexual relationship. And other challenges of their life together lined up and waited to be tackled. Now living squarely in present time, however, instead of hovering between theaters of past and present, they were able to do just that.

### EPILOG

Jeremy and Shawna stayed the course. It was a rough road, not quick and not linear. But as they hung in there and did their work, their character and reactions increasingly made sense, even as they were changing. They could see about themselves and each other, "Oh, that is why I was that way." Freed from the tyranny of an unending past and armed with understanding, they could choose to change. It was deeply moving to witness each other's deep work, and they became ever closer in the process while also constructing a picture of themselves and their lives that became organized into a coherent autobiography. Last I heard, they had married and had two little boys. Those two have a good shot at a secure attachment style!

## Chapter Ten

# EMOTIONAL RESCUE: THE TRANSFORMATIVE POWER OF REPAIR

These first 10 chapters, like the first substantial stage of couples therapy, are about relationship work and trauma work. An unjust but undeniable fact of life is that trauma and neglect saddle children and later adults with a dysregulated nervous systems and often steeper-than-average challenges around attachment and relating. In preparing the soil to address the sexual relationship, we must quiet the static-sparked and erratic electricity of triggering. Perhaps your relationship has been like a temperamental cell phone in the mountains that breaks up or even cuts out in certain pockets of terrain. The ground under a rewarding sexual relationship is a steady and reliable connection. Creating that is no small feat! Yet in many cases, once we have gotten this far, the work of the sexual relationship is the home stretch with the heaviest lifting already behind us.

Before transitioning to sex, I want to reiterate that disagreement, conflict, and even anger are natural parts of life. Much as my partner has no interest in ever being my identical twin or clone (I don't know why!), I doubt if yours will either. So our mission throughout the life of the relationship, should we decide to accept it, is to disagree or express our anger nondefensively and with respect. We cannot eradicate lapses of disharmony, but we can make of them a nonevent or simply a hiccup rather than a catastrophe. This requires learning and utilizing swift and effective repair skills. A world in which a misstep or mistake is fatal is a wildly dangerous one! The possibility of repair transforms that high-stakes, pressured world into a safer one, because in effect you have more than one chance.

A child growing up with trauma or neglect has little or no experience with repair. That child was hurt and left alone to work it out. For many, if they cried, that made matters far worse; rather than comfort they were then given "something to cry about." There was probably no making sense out of how this could have happened and no assistance in the desperate quest to recover and come back into connection. An apology was probably on the order of a fantastic dream. These children may have never learned what to do in such inevitable and thus terrifying moments of rupture.

Children adapt as they can. Some blame themselves for all their woes, agreeing with those who will readily blame them. Some withdraw and hide in confusion and shame. Some escape and find connections elsewhere, maybe never to return to the painful family homestead. Some deny by either forgetting or pretending that anything untoward ever happened. Some tap dance in a tireless attempt to please and appease. All of these and many other possible adaptations, driven by a primal and biological drive to be attached, are the best a child can come up with, an effort to survive. They persist into adult relationship until if we are lucky, effective repair skills can be learned.

What follows is one repair tool to assist during the "threadbare rug" stage and as needed, beyond. I hope it will become part of an armamentarium of healing software and hardware. More than once I have had clients request, "Please send me the electronic version of the Life Boat so I can put it in my phone and keep it with me for whenever I might need it!" I am always happy to do so.

## ENTER THE LIFE BOAT: A SAFE PASSAGE TO TERRA FIRMA

The Life Boat is a repair tool for those times when both partners are triggered, distraught, feeling trapped in disconnection, and seeing themselves begin to lift off into the wild pitch of escalation. They may be panicking, saying to each other or desperately thinking, "How do we get out of here?" Although I am not a fan of cute acronyms, clients do describe feeling very much as if they are drowning in these conflicts, and emerging from them is something on the order of getting to shore alive. It is worth remembering the steps. So I hope the acronym helps.

| Life | B | —— | O | —— | A | —— | T |
|------|---|----|---|----|---|----|---|
|      | I |    | W |    | P |    | O |
|      | D |    | N |    | P |    | U |
|      |   |    |   |    | R |    | C |
|      |   |    |   |    | E |    | H |
|      |   |    |   |    | C |    |   |
|      |   |    |   |    | I |    |   |
|      |   |    |   |    | A |    |   |
|      |   |    |   |    | T |    |   |
|      |   |    |   |    | E |    |   |

## The Steps

**1. The Bid**: B is for *Bid*, a term from the Gottman lexicon, meaning a gesture or overture of contact. In this case, the bid is when one partner has the presence of mind to initiate or suggest the activity of repair. This could be done by saying, "I'd like to propose a Life Boat, is this a good time?" Mutual agreement to engage in the activity and on the timing is *essential,* as often a feeling of coercion or powerlessness is part of the conflict dynamic.

When one partner makes the bid, the other may be not quite ready at that moment, perhaps needing to calm down more before engaging at all. If that is the case, and it is fine if it is, that partner is instructed to be very specific about *when* the soonest good time might be.

The "B" is also a reminder of the body and the breath. Remember that breath is a primary resource for self-regulation. The exhalation is key in activating the parasympathetic process of settling and calming. Slowing the breath with a mindful focus on the out breath is an invaluable practice!

**2. Ownership**: O is for *Ownership*, which is taking responsibility for your contribution to the escalation/conflict. Our assumption is that it *always* takes two to escalate. Even if one partner "started it," as little children are always quick to point out, if the other does not react or overreact, there will be no escalation. The activity of ownership is a sharing of responsibility for the creation of both the problem and the solution. And it is in effect an apology.

One of the advantages of the Life Boat is that it insures that ownership will be shared. Often I find partners hesitate to take the high road of ownership or apology because they fear they will wind up being blamed for the whole thing or because they bitterly complain that the other partner "*never*" owns or apologizes.

In the Life Boat, equal ownership is built into the structure, making it safer to practice humility and self-reflection.

The protocol recommends two "rounds" of ownership, but often more are required. A round is where partners take turns, one item each time, owning one piece of the conflict. Again, because the paradigm is "no blame," owning your own piece does *not* mean the whole thing is your fault!

And what do we mean by ownership? It is specific and concrete, it is what I *did* (a *specific* action or verbalization) that made things worse for us and that I honestly regret. Detail helps, but it is preferable not to be wordy. Wordiness might appear defensive, and when both partners are in a charged-up emotional state, clarity, precision, and sincerity are of the utmost significance, as is avoiding language that might reincite conflict. We want to avoid that either partner monopolize, but rather, keep the process moving. Including an actual apology can be most powerful! An example might be:

> One thing I can own is that I was impatient and repeated my words with a sharp, nasty tone when you could not hear me. I am sorry for that.

What ownership is not:

Ownership is not explaining.
Ownership is not excuses.
Ownership is not a veiled way of saying, "You triggered me!"
Ownership is not implying, "I only did what I did because of what *you* did"
Ownership is not a trick to coerce counterownership!

In order to be potent, ownership must be honest and heartfelt. Your partner can surely smell if it is not! Both partners are encouraged to be mindful that their tone and facial expression are congruent with the intention of repair, both in the sender and the receiver roles. Strive to be a patient and respectful listener, even if your partner does not own or begin by owning what *you* see as his or her worst transgression. Expressing disappointment or a critique of how your partner is performing in the process will undoubtedly sink it!

After two rounds of ownership, see what you notice and how each of you feels. A good reference point is the state of the body. If breath has deepened and the body of each partner is more relaxed and open, you are making progress. If there is still tension and shallow breath or a tight, constricted feeling remains in the body of either or both of you, there are more rounds to be done. In particularly gnarly situations, you are likely to decide to do more. Either partner can request this. It is preferable for each partner to do the same number of rounds.

As receiver, monitor your reaction to your partner's expression of ownership. It is difficult to stay present when you are very hurt and when your partner does not immediately address the piece that hurt you the most. Continue to use your breath. It may just take a little longer to get there.

Know that you can enhance the depth and healing potential of the process by staying in your own yard and going deeper and further *yourself*. As ever in relationship work, we want to teach self-reflection rather than blame, self- rather than other-focus.

**3. Appreciation:** A is for *Appreciation*. In order to be stable, we now know that a relationship requires a positive-to-negative ratio of five-to-one. Expressions of admiration and appreciation are a vitally important relationship element, and most likely in the stage of high conflict, you are sorely in the red. Appreciation can be one of the most potent mechanisms for emerging from the howling tempest into connection. For one thing, the appreciated partner has the experience of being *seen* in some way, and seen in a positive light. In light of the age-old shame template, it makes sense that an expression of appreciation would be powerful, especially in times of triggered distress. The communication of "You see good in me" might counteract the persistent belief "What I have done is irreversible and who I am unforgivable."

The appreciation step also benefits the "sending" partner in that "remembering something good about you makes me feel less like a loser for staying in the relationship with you." (Of course you would not say that, but many people are thinking it in these moments!)

Take turns doing two (or more) rounds of appreciations, each round expressing one thing you appreciate about your partner. It is ideal to have the appreciations be related to the conflict or to the ownership process, but that is not essential. What is essential is that the appreciation be *personal*. Specificity, depth, heartfelt feeling, and brevity all make for healing, potent appreciations. Again, both partners should be thoughtful and cautious not to retrigger one another with barbed or ambiguous expressions! Rather, strive to be gracious, openhearted and generous in both giving and receiving. Remember, we are trying to get back together!

**4. Touch:** For many partners, touch is more connecting than words. So to end the process with some sort of caring touch integrates that component into the repair. It could be a hug, a stroke of the partner's face or arm, a squeeze of the hand. This may not be acceptable to everyone, but I encourage it. See what feels most natural to the two of you. I like it when each partner offers a touch, so each has the important experience of both offering and accepting (which is something it seems we are always working on). Touch can be soothing, boost serotonin and oxytocin, and serve as an antidote to depression and rupture if it is safe for both partners.

After finishing all the steps, see how you each feel inside, emotionally and physically, and notice how it feels between you. The whole process usually takes under half an hour. I suggest that you let some time pass before returning to the topic that produced the original conflict. Most likely some time later you will be able to talk about it calmly, utilizing what each of you learned from the Life Boat.

Remember, the Life Boat is *not* designed to process what that original conflict was about but rather to get you safely to the terra firma of reconnection. I suggest you practice it some time when you are not triggered to get familiar with the sequence, like a fire drill. Then it will be in your toolkit ready to use should you need it. Again, even in the best of relationships, some measure of conflict is inevitable. There is no shame in needing to go back and use this tool should you need to. Not often, but once in a great while, I still need to dust it off and fire it up. When we do, I am glad it is still there where we tucked it away for safekeeping.

## SUMMING UP

The human brain is minimally formed at birth. If it were to mature fully in utero, the child's head would probably grow so large as to kill the mother in the push to be born. So after birth the brain continues to form and build new structures and connections, approaching some semblance of "completion" by our late 20s. Even thercafter, however, new neurons and new connections between neurons may continue to sprout until our last breaths. We can learn from experience, which in fact changes the structure of the brain all of our lives. I view relationship in much the same way. When we first partner, the nascent relationship has the rough beginnings of what is required to function together. Much care and feeding—food and water, rest and exercise, and plenty of education and practice—are required to reach relationship "maturity."

I always tell single people who are looking for their "ideal" life partner (or anyone else who will listen!) that there is really only one nonnegotiable factor in mate selection. *Find someone who is willing to work on relationship through the lifespan. With that, you will be fine.* You can put that on my tombstone! A good relationship, like a good brain, is a work in progress, forever! Ours is a culture of throwing out the old and ever seeking the novel and improved or updated version. For many it is a foreign concept that continued effort in relationship may be evidence of health and growth rather than an indicator that this is the "wrong" relationship. And apology, rather being a show of weakness or defeat, may be a grand demonstration of courage and strength.

Part III

# INTRODUCTION TO THE WIDE WORLD OF SEX

## Chapter Eleven

# THE LEGACY OF RABBI HILLEL: THE NATURE OF SEX

As a little girl I learned a story about Rabbi Hillel, a Talmudic scholar and sage living some time around the first century. As the story goes, a skeptic challenged him, pointedly demanding, "Rabbi, tell us the essence of Torah while standing on one foot." Rabbi Hillel did not hesitate, perched on one foot he replied,

> If I am not for myself, who will be for me?
> And if I am only for myself, what good am I?
> If not now, when?
> All the rest is but commentary.
> Now go and study!

Having heard it so many times, I even remember the famous quote in Hebrew. Some years ago as an adult I heard the story again, and it dawned on me: Rabbi Hillel may have been the first sex therapist! What he was teaching, besides being the essence of Torah, is in fact the essence of good sex! In order for sex to be satisfying, a sexual partner must be present to his or her *own* experience, present to the experience of the *other* partner, and in the *present moment.*

All the rest is icing. I say, now go and practice!

Most children of trauma and neglect never learned the fundamentals about sex and sexuality; or, through distorted, haphazard, or cataclysmic experience, they pieced together whatever their understanding of sex came to be. This chapter will attempt to provide some fundamentals about a decidedly enormous topic.

Before we begin, however, one important sidebar: Although trauma and neglect undoubtedly complicate sexual life and often make of it anything from a challenge to a protracted nightmare, many aspects of what our couples struggle with are well within the range of countless generic couples of every ilk. So without any intention of minimizing the pain, I do wish to some extent to "normalize" or destigmatize the difficulties and suffering of survivor couples. Since most men and women do not go around talking openly about their sexual difficulties or dysfunctions, everyone is prone to believe "Nobody else has them except me." So far from the truth!

## SEXUAL HEALTH

In 1972, select representatives of 60 countries, under the auspices of the World Health Organization, assembled to craft a definition of sexual health. It took them many weeks of laborious debate to hammer it out. Well beyond the absence of illness or injury, sexual health is multifaceted and laden in its diverse characteristics and meanings. It is shaped by culture, morality, politics, economics, religion, aesthetics, reproductive norms, the march of history, and more. In 2009, they returned to the table to update their files. (Those interested can read their definitions in the archives of the WHO or even the 2002 U.S. Surgeon General's Report.)

I only mention this as a reminder that what we each identify or strive for as our own sexual relationship ideal can have as many possible forms as the world is wide. First with ourselves and then with our partners, it behooves us to do what that patient and persistent committee has done: define our terms and elaborate a vision.

## HOW DID IT BEGIN?

Ideally, parents would be good sex educators as children progress through the developmental stages, each stage studded with mystery and curiosity. Unfortunately, this is rarely the case, at least in our culture, fraught as it is with chaotic, mixed messages about sex. When there is childhood sexual abuse, the messages are all the more contorted and incomprehensible to children; when there is neglect, the child is cast out into the void to figure it out or find answers somehow (which also makes that child more vulnerable to abuse).

Returning to our exploration of attachment styles, we might superimpose the overlay of sexual development onto the attachment trajectory. Beginning around the age of 2, children begin to notice their genitals and, like with everything else, become curious about them as a source of play and pleasure.

Of course it is natural to want to look and touch, just as at this stage it is natural that most *anything* is a toy, and most likely goes straight in the mouth! These little ones need care, support, and safe boundaries for their exploration. Viewing the emergence of body awareness through the lens of developing attachment patterns offers much food for thought, to which we shall return later.

As children become a little older, they begin to notice and think about gender and gender identity. They are fascinated with who is a girl and who is a boy and what they themselves are. They might become quite interested in both Mommy's and Daddy's bodies and how they are different from each other's and from "mine." Again, the curiosity is most natural. Again, as they pursue their innate explorations, they must be watched and guided, oriented, and kept safe. What do you imagine about the budding sexual development of the various attachment styles: the avoidantly attached? the anxious ambivalent? the disorganized disoriented? How do you imagine attachment styles affect the shape of emerging sexuality, even apart from any untoward life events?

As they grow, go to school, and have peers and friends, children are still more aware of gender. Depending on their culture, they might be treated in specific ways that shape or dictate their developing gender identities. They will certainly be inspired to compare notes with each other. Some children now have the good fortune to have parents who answer their questions and help them find their own way. Sadly, that is still, for the most part, the exception.

What do you remember about your early years of life? What do you remember noticing or thinking about your own body? What messages did you receive at home or at school about gender? About touch? What was the response to your curiosity or your questions? Was it even OK to ask questions or talk about such things? What kinds of words were used to refer to body parts, if they were spoken of at all? Do you remember any feelings about your own body or the bodies of others? Or is it all a blank?

With puberty, havoc breaks loose in the bodies of both genders. These young people watch their bodies morph before their wide eyes, and beyond the visible, they helplessly observe changes in function, sensation, and emotion. They even smell and sound different to themselves. And they might be visited by new and confounding, even perhaps frightening impulses and urges. They might be visited by dreams and fantasies and feelings about others that are different, highly stimulating, even exciting. And all this at a developmental time that is centered on identity formation.

What do you remember about your own changing body? What was it like seeing and feeling it change? What did you receive in the way of sex education? Was your developing maturity a source of joy and celebration or cause for shame and hiding? What were the messages you got about becoming a sexual being? How did you feel about it yourself? Was there anyone you could talk to? Where, if anywhere, could you go for information?

It is also natural for young people to encounter the mystery of masturbation. For some it can be an exciting, empowering experience of discovery, perhaps of autonomy and control. For others it may be an embarrassment or a sin. What do you remember about it? What messages did you receive from your family, friends, and community about masturbation? And what did you make of those messages? Did you learn it was OK to talk about sex? If so, with whom? And what sort of language did you use to talk about it? What about body image? What do you remember thinking and feeling about your changing body? What were the messages you received about that?

These early and formative experiences are the canvas upon which later life events were painted, the context or environment surrounding whatever else did or did not occur. And they are the foundation upon which subsequent and ultimately adult relationships emerged and took shape. Considering them is part of the process of creating a coherent autobiography. Verbalizing and sharing them with your partner can be a powerful and intimate way to be more deeply known to each other. What would that be like?

## Chapter Twelve

# THIS THING CALLED LOVE: MYTHS AND FACTS ABOUT ADULT SEXUALITY

The culture and media give us a glorious picture of the kind of sex everyone else must be having. "Perfect" bodies, always hot and always ready, instantaneous rock-hard erections, copious and immediate lubrication, loud and simultaneous chandelier-swinging orgasms, right? That is the "norm," according to Hollywood, that most of us have grown up comparing ourselves to, never really knowing what is "normal." The most typical question a sex therapist hears is, "Is this normal? My partner wants to do such and such . . . I have fantasized about such and such . . . Is this normal? Or is there something terribly wrong or perverse about him, her, me?" That is the purpose of this chapter, to provide the gentle and candid sex education that most of us never had, or at least the beginnings of it. This section is generic and does not yet address the special considerations around trauma and neglect. And because many traumatized people have managed to stay clear of sexual relating their whole lives and therefore are not versed in the basics, this chapter provides those.

## I'M CRAZY ON YOU: THE PEA EFFECT

I learned about PEA from one of my greatest teachers and mentors, Pat Love. Here is how it works. Nature's priority being the preservation of the species, we are evolutionarily designed to be turned on to the same person long enough to procreate. (No matter what our sexual orientation is, we are all the same in this.) So at the beginning of a relationship, the brains and bodies of both partners begin to pump a high-potency biochemical cocktail consisting of the neuropeptide phenethylamine (PEA), the neurotransmitters dopamine and serotonin, testosterone, and other naturally produced endogenous intoxicants. Most of us know what the effect of this feels like. Libido is spiked, so a person with a naturally low libido feels more readily aroused and maybe even walks around feeling turned on. A naturally high-libido person might feel, "Ah . . . At last I've met my match." We go without sleep and don't get tired; sex is endlessly interesting, fun, and unusually frequent. While "under the influence," we may find ourselves wanting to be with the person or just daydreaming about being together much of the time. We are blind to most flaws and may even lose weight as our hunger is directed elsewhere. Do you remember what I am describing? Harville Hendrix and some other relationship experts refer to this stage as the "romantic love" stage because the emotional and mental states that accompany this chemistry are thick with the poetry, gesture, and symbolism of intense romance.

Unfortunately, nature's plan is reproduction and not necessarily long-term relationship. After somewhere between 3 and 18 months, our biochemistry returns to its natural baseline and the drug effect wears off. At this point, couples not forewarned that it is a universally time-limited state may look at each other and wonder, "Where did it go?" They may feel as if the magic has slipped away. Perhaps the heat of desire wanes, sagging libidos return, some even think, "I love you but I'm not 'in love' with you anymore." Some couples break up at this stage. Many stay together and the relationship difficulties set in.

My observation over several decades of working with trauma and neglect couples is that the "PEA effect" (my shorthand for the whole biochemical high) overrides the trauma and neglect relationship and sexual symptomatology. Most of the couples I have seen over the years can look back on some brief period at the beginning of their relationship when the sex was plentiful, fluid, free of triggering, even hot and satisfying. What is most important to know is that it is natural for the comparative ease and heightened desire to recede. Sadly, this is a chemically enhanced state, which is not to say that we cannot re-create hot, satisfying, and plentiful sex again, but that particular state is by its nature and purpose brief, fleeting, and a one-time deal for everyone.

Many find it helpful to know that this relationship stage is both universal and normal, so although perhaps it's disappointing, it is not tragic when it ends and is certainly not a death knell to the relationship. And for those couples whose relationship is later complicated by trauma and neglect dynamics, I think knowing about PEA demystifies the time when perhaps things were easier.

## START ME UP: THE TRUTH ABOUT SEXUAL DESIRE

In the 1950s, a generation of bold researchers began to study and write about human sexuality. It was radical to make of sex a scientific enterprise and to begin to discuss openly what people did in bed. Sex therapy arrived on the scene as a new helping profession to assist couples with difficulties, and both a clinical and popular literature slowly emerged alongside it. A staple appearing in this literature was the sexual response cycle, which mapped the natural sequence of stages of a sexual event. According to that map, which has persisted more than half a century, the first phase of the cycle is known as desire.

Certainly adolescent boys walk around much of the time with a gnawing hunger in the groin and the accompanying thoughts and emotions. Generally they have little need for a stimulus to activate it! Few of the rest of us experience sexual desire quite like that. Sexual desire is largely determined by testosterone levels in all genders. There is a wide range of possible levels, as with all sorts of genetic traits. Generally, desire correlates to how frequently the individual would want to engage in sexual activity of some kind.

The norm in couples with or without any sort of sexual difficulties is that desire levels are discrepant, meaning not a match. I recall the split-screen scene in an old Woody Allen movie where on one side of the screen, Woody whines, "We *hardly ever* have sex! Only about three times a week!" On the other side of the screen is his exhausted partner exclaiming, "*All we do* is have sex! We have sex three times a week!" Some people believe it is an aspect of evolutionary design that higher- and lower-libido people wind up together: If too many low-testosterone people paired up, it might compromise the preservation of the species. What is important to know is that in most couples, there is a higher- and a lower-libido person, and they may have frustrations or judgments about each other's desire level if it causes conflict between them. There is no norm, no right or wrong, no universal standard of "health" about desire level. Like height and eye color, it just varies. And depending on how discrepant they are, partners find a way to work it out.

In the year 2000, some important new research appeared. After the 50-year reign of the old sexual response cycle, we learned that for a large percentage of men and women, the first stage is *not* desire. That is to say, physical and emotional arousal do *not* necessarily precede and thus provide the impetus for sexual activity. But stimulation of some kind can awaken it, and a satisfying time can be had by all. This is good news for the countless individuals who feared, "There is something wrong with me because I never feel horny" or who imagine that in order to have successful sex, one must come to the table already turned on. Not so! It is also good news for the partners of those people, especially if they take the time to learn about what sort of stimulation works to awaken desire. When the heart is willing, with attention, intention, and care, the body can be inspired to follow.

## IMAGINE: ABOUT FANTASY

The world of sexual fantasy is rich, elaborately textured, and deeply personal. The content of fantasy can be as wildly varied as the world is wide. Psychologists have correlated erotic fantasies to early life experiences, attachment history, and peak sexual experiences. Some couples find it intimate and exciting to share them or even enact them together. There are a few things about sexual fantasy that I think are useful knowledge.

Early in the twenty-first century, a British sex researcher did a most amazing piece of work. He interviewed thousands of American and English adults of widely ranging ages, demographics, and orientations and compiled an impressive body of work about just what is going on in people's heads about and during sex. He found that a vast percentage of women and men regularly fantasize about people *other* than their partners and imagine doing things they would never do *with* their partners. This is utterly typical and normative. Generally they have no intention of ever realizing the fantasy, but rather it is an enhancement or aphrodisiac to the sex they are actually having, whether alone or with the partner.

Alice, in her early 60s, struggled with self-conscious angst about body image as she aged. It was hard for her to hear or believe her partner Charlie's compliments and positive exclamations about her body. He was still very attracted to her, turned on by her, and unquestionably devoted to her. Yet she could not get over the fact that he had sexual fantasies about Jennifer Lopez. Resigned to never being able to compete with JLo, she found herself rather jealously ashamed and hiding from Charlie. Even though Charlie had no intention of pursuing his fantasy in actual life, Alice felt threatened and inadequate.

In a therapy session, we discussed the research on sexual fantasy. She was surprised to hear how common and minimally significant it is for men or women to fantasize "outside the relationship." She also admitted she had been hot for Mick Jagger for 40 years, much longer than she had even known Charlie. It was a revelation to her that Charlie's feelings about JLo were not very different from her feelings about Mick and no more of a threat to the relationship. Just this little bit of information helped shift something in terms of her acceptance of both herself and Charlie.

Granted, some religions hold that fantasy is tantamount to committing the imagined acts. If that is your belief system, it of course changes this discussion.

## NIGHT IN MY VEINS: OXYTOCIN

Oxytocin is another naturally occurring chemical in the body. It is the bonding chemical. In order to insure that mothers take appropriate care of their young, nature designed a chemical that would bond them together. It is secreted most notably in nursing mothers. Oxytocin also functions to bond lovers. In women it is secreted upon penetration and with orgasm. In men, interestingly, it is secreted when a man falls asleep after an orgasm!

This is useful information for a number of reasons. Many women are distressed by their connection to the perpetrator of their sexual abuse. It upsets them to feel so tied to someone who harmed them in that way; they may also feel shame and guilt about such feelings. "I feel so attached to him. Does that make the sexual abuse my fault? Or am I some kind of masochist?"

It is also important in that it reminds us, "Don't have sex with someone you don't really like!" That could result in confusing conflict between emotions and the body, with the heart saying, "Get me out of here!" and the body saying "I want to be close to you! I want more of you!"

Finally, and this may be most important for our purposes, regular lovemaking really is good for the relationship. Eileen said, "We've all been told or perhaps noticed that women want to feel connected *before* having sex and that men get connected *through* having sex. I always believed that and often when I felt disconnected from Rich, I just did not want to have sex. I noticed that when we had sex, Rich was in a better mood or maybe was nicer to me, so I began sometimes having sex because of that. I made an interesting discovery, however, about *myself*. After we had sex *I also felt closer to him*. I started to stretch a little more when I thought I didn't feel amorous, because I knew it was good for me and good for us!"

## I FEEL THE EARTH MOVE: ABOUT ORGASM

There is so much mythology about the "Big O." If we only got our sex education from the movies, we'd imagine that it is typical to have spine-chilling, shrieking, simultaneous orgasms during every sexual act. This is hardly the norm. Many men have reliable orgasms; not all women have had them yet at all. Sexology pioneer Betty Dodson has been teaching women how to have orgasms both in group workshops and in individual sessions for about 50 years for that very reason. Orgasm is definitely something that women can learn, and no it is not always "just natural" and easy for women to come. If you haven't quite gotten there yet, if you only do sometimes, or if it takes you a while to come, you are not alone!

Freud believed that "mature" female orgasms were vaginal, that is, stimulated in the vagina and preferably by intercourse. We now know that a majority of women are stimulated to orgasm via the clitoris, a small penis-like internal organ teeming with nerve endings, which serves no other known purpose. A significant percentage of women require some clitoral stimulation to have an orgasm, and clitoral orgasms are much more the norm than the touted vaginal ones. It is relatively uncommon for women to have orgasms during intercourse without some additional stimulation. As for orgasms in ringing unison, that is also far from the norm. Some partners come together or close, others do not. Some women and men need much more time and perhaps a fair amount of "help" to get off. And not everyone has an orgasm every time.

It is just important to know that if one partner (or both) does not have an orgasm, it is nobody's fault! In fact, it is not a point of guilt or shame. Many partners worry if the other does not come. "Maybe he's not attracted to me!" "Maybe I'm not a good enough lover!" That kind of anxiety puts more pressure on the partner who did not come and may make the sexual encounter something like a performance or spectator event rather than an opportunity to be close. Furthermore, anxiety is vasoconstricting, which means the body, arteries, and veins tense and tighten, inhibiting blood flow. Engorgement, erection, and arousal are all about blood flow, so vasoconstriction begins to choke them out.

I teach people that we are all responsible for our own orgasm, and sometimes you may not even necessarily want to have one. For individuals whose natural testosterone level is on the lower side, coming to orgasm may take a significant amount of concentration and effort. At times it might feel like "work" and just not seem worth it. That is certainly their prerogative and may make sense, especially if they are tired or preoccupied.

Although orgasms may be wonderfully pleasurable and release a lot of calming and soothing natural chemicals in the body, they are not the only reason to have sex. And many couples very happily have satisfying and intimate sexual rendezvous without any orgasms at all. That may be a hard sell, but believing that a splendid time can be had by all, with or without orgasm, can take a lot of the pressure off, especially as we get older!

Nicola had never had an orgasm and her partner Jan was vociferously disappointed about that. Jan missed the turn-on of watching Nicola come and also felt inadequate, asking, "What am I not doing? What am I doing wrong?" Jan's harping on it and also taking it personally made Nicola's nonorgasm into a problem. Nicola felt incompetent, bad about herself, and as if she were a sexual disappointment to Jan.

There is a difference between ejaculation and orgasm for men. Ejaculation is the emission of semen from the penis. Orgasm is the sensory experience, the body feeling. One can happen without the other, especially due to illness or aging.

Orgasms may wax and wane through the lifespan. Hormones may fluctuate through the month, around pregnancy, and with age. Many medications affect arousal and orgasms, and not all doctors think to warn or advise their patients about this. Or doctors may believe that the benefit of their medicine is a reasonable tradeoff for your pleasure or orgasm. Mood states can also affect arousal and orgasm. Depression and anxiety can readily quench the spark, as can alcohol and recreational drugs. Given that we are all different, there is a vast world of knowledge to be acquired and exchanged about the nature and ecology, "care and feeding" of your own and your partner's orgasm.

## I TOUCH MYSELF: MASTURBATION

Woody Allen is famous for describing masturbation as "having sex with someone I love." Although we did make mention of masturbation as it features in earlier sexual development, it is worth revisiting because of the wide range of possible attitudes that partners may have about it. For some people, it is strictly sanctioned by their religious or moral code, viewed simply and clearly as "wrong." For others, masturbation continues to be a source of pleasure, tension relief, or a way to bridge the desire gap between discrepant partners throughout the life of the relationship. When the relationship is not going well, masturbation may in fact feel like the only way to have sex with someone who likes you or may just be much less stressful. For some couples, masturbation is something to share: to do in each other's presence or to offer one another. To some partners it is a source of guilt, shame, or suspicion, almost like cheating, as sex is viewed as something reserved only for the partner.

What are your beliefs and attitudes about masturbation? Does your partner know your beliefs and attitudes? Do you know your partner's? Do you masturbate? Does your partner know? Do you know if your partner masturbates? How do you feel about that? Would you be jealous if your partner's masturbation included pictures, vibrators, or sex toys? What would it be like to discuss this with your partner?

There are no right or wrong answers about this. What is crucial is that both partners feel free and accepted, understanding and understood.

## WHEN I'M 64: SEXUALITY THROUGH THE LIFESPAN

Until less than 100 years ago, the average lifespan was around 40. Having children met important economic needs for working family farms and businesses and caring for elders who were too old to work themselves any longer. The mandate to be fruitful and multiply persisted as a reason to have sex, and adults did not live long after their childbearing years.

Twentieth- and twenty-first-century couples can look forward to three or more decades after menopause of monogamous sexual life with no intent to procreate. My grandparents and perhaps yours probably did not need books on sex after menopause or erection-enhancing drugs. Sustaining passion and interest over many years in a monogamous sexual relationship whose only functions are pleasure and intimacy is a wholly contemporary challenge. As a culture, we are failing pretty miserably if we look at statistics about divorce and affairs.

After the PEA-spiked romantic love stage, there follows a sequence of expectable other stages that influence sexuality. Pregnancy and the transition to parenthood dramatically change the entire landscape of daily life, and researchers say that on the average, "marital satisfaction drops by 70% with the birth of the first child." Between sleep deprivation, fatigue, lack of time and privacy, major hormonal shifts, and body changes, sexuality can take a hit. For some couples, it may take a long time to recover.

Obviously as we get older our bodies change. Testosterone levels in both genders can recede significantly, potentially changing libido levels. For men, erections may be unreliable, less solid, and more difficult to sustain. In women, vaginal dryness and the natural thinning of the vaginal wall may make intercourse more difficult or even painful. Orgasm may be elusive or take longer to attain. And aging bodies may not look like JLo or Mick anymore, producing self-consciousness or fear. All of these changes are natural and universal consequences of living longer. How do we cope with them?

There are many books, DVDs, and experts around now to help answer that question. The bibliography of this book will name a few. What is important now is simply to know that these are expectable and usual facts of relationship life for all of us, calling for creativity, compassion, and good communication. Many couples find in later life that the necessities of contraception, preoccupation, and distraction of kids and even work give way to space and time. They truly know each other after many years. This mature love may be the deepest and most satisfying they have ever known.

## SATISFACTION: RESEARCH ABOUT LONG-TERM "GOOD SEX"

In 2005 sex therapist, scholar, and researcher Peggy Kleinplatz surveyed thousands of self-identified long-term, monogamous couples with satisfying, happy sex lives. She was looking for the ingredients of lasting passion. Kleinplatz's research showed six items that scored the highest on most of the couples' lists. At the top of the list was *presence*: being in the moment and attuned to the emotions and body of both self and other. Presence by its nature takes partners out of the realm of performance and its attendant self-consciousness and self-focus and more into a zone of related exchange and rapport. It also takes the emphasis off outcome (no pun intended!) or orgasm, which as we age may not necessarily happen every time. With presence, the meaning of the encounter is being together in pleasurable and relaxed communion. Being truly relaxed elicits joy, and to share a deep calm is to share joy.

The second most highly valued element was *authenticity*: being emotionally and physically real and visible. Being authentic is to allow your partner to know and do what *actually has an impact*, so it involves opening yourself to the other, giving over some power, vulnerability, and trust. All of this makes for a deep intimate moment.

The third highly valued ingredient is *intense connection in the moment*, which is of course implied by the first two. This is where all the work partners have done together, all the familiarity of time spent in a life shared, may be money in the bank of being truly known to one another (although it may also be possible with a shorter time of knowing each other). The point is that the power of the interaction is in the *sharing* of the moment, not in the good time experienced by one or the other.

The fourth component was *intimacy*, both emotional and erotic: feeling cherished, respected, valued as a person by both self and partner, and also feeling desirable and desired.

The fifth point on the list is *communication*. In Kleinplatz's words, "These people are black belt communicators," both in words and in touch, in general and about the sexual relationship in particular.

The final point, more difficult to describe, is *transcendence*; or some sort of spiritual connection in the shared experience.

None of the top six characteristics on the long-term sexual satisfaction list requires looking like a porn star or having the athleticism or stamina of a 19-year-old. It is not about technique or ingenuity, but maturity and love. This sounds like a pretty wonderful journey into old age to me!

Kleinplatz's research and Rabbi Hillel have much in common. And both omitted to explicitly name a foundational and central pillar of the structure of a successful intimate life: boundary. In order to be truly intimate, there must be two distinct and connected beings. Eroticism and what makes sex exciting and interesting is the curiosity about contrast and mystery, the interface between the known and the not known, self and other. Trauma and neglect rob the individual of this. With neglect, there is no other with whom to attach and explore. With trauma, there is in effect no self to be, the self having been somehow subsumed by the trauma or the traumatizing other(s). All of our trauma work and relationship work seeks to build and grow this boundary of self, and therefore all that work is in service of the eroticism and sexual work that is to follow. So let's go on!

Chapter Thirteen

# I'M BAD TO THE BONE: TRAUMA AND SEXUALITY

Whenever mind, emotions, the body, and relationship all interface in one activity or experience, a behemoth of catalytic convergence results. These essential force fields of human existence together function like the cherries on a slot machine. When the cherries all line up, their harmonious confluence can produce a compelling and life-changing jackpot that keeps you coming back for more. When they don't, the disharmony may generate a nagging, unrelenting, and costly preoccupation that will not stay in Vegas. Sexuality, perhaps like nothing else, is a mighty meeting place of these most consequential aspects of our being. We now know that trauma is such a meeting place as well. When the trauma is sexual, we can assume that it touches every area of a person's being. This is good news and bad. The good news is that we have many access routes for healing. The more challenging news is that in order to be successful, healing must address the whole person. This chapter will describe some common sexual difficulties experienced by many women and men with trauma histories. Some may sound familiar to you. Some may not. Not everyone struggles with all of them!

At the core of trauma is a profound experience of helplessness and of being worthless or insignificant. This is true whether the trauma is a rape or an earthquake. There is no stopping the powerful approaching, overwhelming force. And that force, whatever it is, does not care how the victim feels. Because helplessness is an utterly unbearable human emotion, we will do anything in our power to avoid feeling it.

One defense against helplessness is guilt: the irrational belief that "there *is* something I could have done, I just didn't do it." Even though guilt is not much fun either, we seem to prefer it to the frightening and contemptible reality that there was in fact *nothing* we could do. Guilt is a ready default and is often reinforced by a blaming world. Historically traumatized veterans were typically blamed and viewed as cowardly; abuse and rape victims were accused of being seductive or "asking for it." Shame and guilt are some of the most persistent emotional by-products of trauma and abuse and can readily evolve into self-hatred and a sense of integral "badness."

## BELIEFS: "I DON'T MATTER"

Not surprisingly, the signature belief of the traumatized is "I don't matter." Julie, for one, was plagued by this gnawing belief. Although she was awesomely smart, a talented athlete, professionally highly regarded, and prominent, her relationships were stormy and often short lived. As a child she was beaten almost daily by her father. No one ever intervened or tried to protect her. As soon as she was able, she ran away. By her own tireless and heroic efforts, she had succeeded in making a life for herself. Now in her middle 40s, she was trying to make a go of an intimate partnership perhaps for the first time. She was tired of the loneliness of her existence.

Julie naturally interpreted people's behavior through the lens of her beliefs about herself and others. She viewed relationship skittishly and defensively. She understood interest and attention from others as their wanting to use or take advantage of her. Any sexual attraction to her was highly suspect, and consequently she had experienced little sex in her life and had increasingly shut down sexually. When I met her, she and Jamie had been partners for 12 years. There had been no sexual relationship between them for more than 10 of those years. Jamie had periodically talked about leaving her because of the absence of sex but had never done so. That was how they happened to come to me.

In Julie's family, the only physical contact had been the violence. When Jamie reached out to touch her, she braced or tensed up as if anticipating a blow. She read Jamie's advances cautiously as if she might be taken advantage of. In general, Julie was somewhat obsessed with "fairness" and an equal give and take. She was so convinced that she did not matter that she was blind to and dismissed many kind and generous things that Jamie did for her. Jamie's random acts of generosity somehow did not register for Julie, or she would find another spin that "proved" Jamie's self-interest or hidden agenda. Although Julie was aware that her self-hatred and negative view of herself were painful to her, she did not see how hurt and insulted Jamie was by being seen and not seen in that way. (We will return to this pattern in Chapter 15.)

Marion, whose trauma was sexual, believed that if she got aroused or had an orgasm, it was evidence that she enjoyed the abuse or caused it by being a slut. She denied or clamped down on any sensation that might be mildly positive or reacted to it with fierce anger. You can imagine what her clamping down and her rage were like for her partner!

## THAT PLACE YOU CAN'T REMEMBER AND YOU CAN'T FORGET: TRAUMATIC RE-EXPERIENCING

Sometimes Julie experienced touch as if it were a flashback of her abuse. A look or an unexpected movement might startle her and it was as if she were back in her family trying to get away from her father. She might wince or contract, erupt in anger, or just leave the room. She was triggered to another time and place just like our Vietnam veteran ducking from the helicopter. It all happened so quickly. Sometimes she experienced a panic response, tightness in her chest, shortness of breath or even inability to breathe, terror, and the thought, "I am going to die!"

Not all trauma survivors experience triggering in such an obvious way. It may be simply that a particular touch, look, or move is extremely, perhaps disproportionally distasteful or unappealing, and it is not immediately clear why. You might just absolutely hate some gesture or interaction, and your partner or even you yourself wonder, "What is the big deal?"

## CAN'T GET IT OUT OF MY HEAD: MORE ABOUT FANTASY

Some survivors of trauma may be distressed about the content of their sexual fantasy. Or they might be worried or confused by who or what turns them on. Julie was decidedly heterosexual and had never had any desire to have sex with women and yet found herself aroused by the Victoria's Secret catalogs that came unsolicited in the mail. She felt ashamed and anxious about what this might mean. I had to reassure her repeatedly that it is quite common and may not necessarily mean anything about sexual orientation for straight people to have dreams, fantasies, or sexual feelings about same-sex people, nor for gay and lesbian people to have similar feelings about the opposite gender.

If the content of your dreams and fantasies frightens you, it can help to talk to a therapist about them. If the trauma was sexual, dreams and fantasies may be retelling the trauma story. In neuroscience-speak, "neurons that fire together wire together." This means that sexual feelings may have gotten coupled or wired in with the trauma memory and continue to be stimulating in the body. The images may be disturbing, and yet they do not mean that you will repeat what was done to you, that you liked it, or that you caused it.

## AS TEARS GO BY: CRYING DURING SEX

One thing that made Julie want to stop having sex with Jamie was her baffling tendency to break into deep sobbing tears during sex. She thought there must be something weird or crazy about her. She was embarrassed and did not know what she was crying about. She worried about upsetting Jamie, but had never dared to inquire about that. Again, I had to reassure her that this is a not uncommon occurrence among traumatized and even nontraumatized people. Sex therapists don't understand it fully. It may very well have to do with making a deep connection with the partner or the self or a profound "letting go" resulting in a cathartic release. We hear about it quite often. Jamie had wondered about it too and mostly wanted to know, "What shall I do if that happens?" Julie only knew she wanted to be held and not asked to explain what's wrong, because she really did not know.

## PAIN

Especially when the trauma was sexual, it is not uncommon to experience some sort of nagging pain syndrome. Julie was apprehensive about beginning any sort of practice including touch because she anticipated pain even if Jamie were to lightly stroke her belly. Her musculature was so tense and braced against assault that even gentle touch, especially if it were unanticipated, hurt, or was irritating at best. She could barely think of a place on her body where it might be safe to begin. She felt somewhat more comfortable if she were doing the touching rather than receiving, perhaps because she felt more in control that way and knew what was going to happen.

Julie had spent her life avoiding her body as much as was humanly possible. Touching herself was the farthest thing from her mind. Julie was unaccustomed to even noticing what she was feeling and rarely even looked in the mirror. Her reflex was to flinch even at the idea. Hers was the pain of fear, tension, and constriction.

It was a revelation to Julie to learn that her breath was her best friend. Deep, intentional breathing with a long exhale was a new experience for her, and she was amazed to discover that she could feel much more comfortable, quickly, doing something that simple. Anxiety is vasoconstricting, which means veins and arteries tighten and narrow, inhibiting blood flow. Relaxation, engorgement, and arousal are all about blood flow. When blood does not flow, energy and positive sensation will not flow either.

Julie learned that by starting out relaxed and agreeing in advance about what was going to happen, she could open to receiving Jamie's touch. At first the pain was somewhat diminished; then it disappeared; and with time she came to find being touched was pleasant and sweet and made her feel closer to Jamie.

I lent Julie a DVD of one of Betty Dodson's workshops. In it a group of women begin the workshop sitting in a circle talking about their personal histories in relation to their bodies and their sexuality. They are all ages, all shapes and sizes, and all of them are naked. Although Julie had to watch the movie slowly, in more than one sitting so as not to get overwhelmed, she was heartened by how many of the women felt much as she had about many things. Laughing, Julie said to me, "Looking at all of them, I suddenly had the guts to look at my own body. I don't look half bad!"

Unfortunately, not all pain syndromes resolve that easily. It is not uncommon that women with trauma histories have more complex pelvic pain problems. Many have been told by health practitioners who cannot find a diagnosable medical explanation, "There is nothing wrong with you," or "It is all in your head." Many have had longstanding vociferous battles with their partners or perhaps been accused that their complaint about pain is a bogus excuse to avoid sex.

*Your pain is real even if its cause is elusive or difficult to pin down.* Thankfully now there is treatment including an emergent physical therapy specialization for both women and men with pelvic pain syndromes. As increasing disciplines and numbers of medical practitioners become understanding and savvy about these problems, they are validated. Guilt, shame, and pain are gently resolved.

## HERE COMES YOUR 19TH NERVOUS BREAKDOWN: COMPULSIVE SEXUAL BEHAVIOR

When Rick first came to me, he was wracked with guilt, shame, and confusion. He was nervous to tell me what brought him to therapy. He was in a committed, monogamous partnership of 6 years. The relationship was extremely important to him. Yet it was not in fact monogamous. Not all the time but periodically, Rick found himself inexplicably and magnetically pulled to bath houses or parks known to be hot spots for anonymous sex. He would seek out an older man and make himself available for a sexual tryst, always himself the desired recipient. Afterward, in disgust and dismay, he would berate himself. He was mystified. "Why am I doing this?" And he was terrified that his partner would find out and he would destroy the relationship. Like a bulimic or alcoholic, he would vow never to do it again—until the next time the urge overtook him.

Over time I learned Rick's story: He had been molested by his beloved grandfather over many years of his childhood. He was repeatedly re-enacting his unprocessed trauma story in the compulsive sexual activity. The shame, confusion, and resolve to stop it that he felt after the episodes in the park or bath house were identical to the feelings he had as a boy about his "dirty secret."

It took a while to penetrate Rick's self-hatred about his behavior by repeatedly explaining to him that *the nature of trauma is to re-enact the trauma.* Since as we know, the cognitive, logical, and verbal part of the brain goes offline during trauma, traumatic memory may be logged in chaotic, fragmented, and impressionistic ways. Disconnected emotions, pain, or patterns of behavior may be desperate attempts at language so the trauma story can somehow be told and processed.

Over time, Rick was able to put his story into words. His previously incomprehensible compulsive sexual behavior was a catalyst, or vehicle, for integration. Bringing together the diverse elements of body sensation, emotion, image, and behavior, making sense of it all, and finding a way to understand the experience and its meaning in the context of the rest of his life story are the ways Rick (or anyone) processed the trauma. Once processed, the trauma memory can be laid to rest. It becomes a quiet chapter in the past like other memory instead of continuing live and flammable in the present. As the attachment researchers have promised us, Rick became infinitely more able to securely attach as a result of putting his life story into a coherent and sequential verbal form.

Although Rick's urges receded significantly as we processed his childhood memories, they did not disappear overnight like in the famous Hitchcock movie where just remembering the trauma was enough to magically and instantly extinguish the problems. Talking to his partner about his urges and developing behavioral strategies to help him resist these urges were other important pieces of our work. Over time Rick successfully stopped the unwanted compulsive activity and, having fulfilled its function, it did not return.

There are other forms of compulsive sexual activity, many not as transparent as Rick's. Some, rather than being traumatic re-enactments, are some sort of desperate attempt at calming down the hyperaroused traumatized nervous system or stimulating a sluggish, numbed-out, traumatized brain. They may be similarly "ego-dystonic," meaning, as they did with Rick, out of step with the rest of a coherent self-image. Similarly, they may be followed by confusion, remorse, guilt, and fear and become hidden. Some compulsive sexual behavior may be truly destructive or harmful to self or others. It may be difficult not to moralize about it. Of course, moralizing or judgment often compound or reinforce the problem, exacerbating the discomfort or self-hatred that the behavior is used to quell, and inciting another cycle of it. The first step is always coming out of hiding and finding the right help.

## NICK OF TIME: A TICKING CLOCK

Sometimes a couple becomes desperate about addressing the sexual relationship because of a time-sensitive desire to have a child. A biological clock may be urgently ticking. It is tricky to try to address traumatized sexuality under the gun. If at all possible, I recommend that couples address the two endeavors separately in order to have a better shot at success with both. Pressure, especially with such delicate and complex challenges, is rarely helpful!

## HOMEWARD BOUND

Although this chapter is not exhaustive and does not present every possible variation on the theme of traumatized sexuality, it may still seem overwhelming. Perhaps your difficulty is an extreme of self-hatred, or self-body hatred; perhaps it is a paralyzing avoidance; perhaps it is a vacuous and unrelenting numbness, or something else still. I remain unabashedly optimistic and hopeful that healing can be accomplished. A willingness to undertake and persist with recovery is the essential ingredient.

Much important personal work occurs during in depth relationship/ couples work. A commitment from both partners is essential, as is an understanding that the work of relationship is a lifelong given and an indicator of a *good* relationship (and probably also a happy life!). Often, however, significant individual work is needed as well. A dysregulated nervous system and a disordered attachment history may necessitate the individual attention that was a core missing childhood experience. Each couple finds its own unique way to map the healing journey.

In closing this chapter on trauma and sexuality, I will reiterate or explicitly state that *your partner is not a helicopter*! The veteran huddled under the bench need not worry about offending, rejecting, or hurting the helicopter's feelings. In your case, there is another person in the relationship. It may be true that you have a terrible story, and there are good reasons that explain your trauma symptoms and your problematic behavior. However, that is not a license or excuse to block out or forget its impact on others. To get lost in your own story and lose sight of the other is in a way repeating what was done to you and replicates your partner's history of abandonment and neglect. However, to get lost in self-hatred about what you are doing to your partner and be swept up in the refrain of "I'm a worthless piece of excrement and I don't deserve you! You'd be much better off without me and I should just die!" is hardly better. I call it going down the rat hole of self-hatred. It is self-centered and abandoning of your partner, and it is still all about you. The great challenge, back to Rabbi Hillel again, is to create authentic, boundaried, and empathic space for both. That is what we want to come home to!

## Chapter Fourteen

# YOU CAN'T ALWAYS GET WHAT YOU WANT: NEGLECT AND SEXUALITY

In resounding *a cappella,* the child of neglect has rewritten the classic song: "You get what you need, *but only when you do it all yourself*!" When I met Art and Stella, both were exhausted, dismayed, and at the verge of hopelessness about their enduring, simmering tension about sex. The sex between them had faded and ultimately stopped more than 5 years prior. Art was quick to say that no less than half the length of their 10-year marriage had been coldly void of sex. Like many couples, they arrived at my door with long-standing repetitive, deeply grooved, and painfully demoralizing patterns of interaction.

Art was a bright, articulate man in his early 40s. Successful in his demanding job in the technology field, he kept busy. He had long hours and a hefty commute. And because he seemed personable and affable, it was not obvious that Stella was one of the few people really in his life. He certainly did not think of himself as particularly lonely or isolated, perhaps just rather "nerdy" and intellectual like many in his field.

Being a bookish sort since childhood, Art had studied quite a bit about Stella's problem. She had been sexually abused for much of her childhood by her alcoholic stepfather. Art had become quite the expert about PTSD and the vast literature on adult children of alcoholics. He believed he understood Stella impeccably well. He was the one who researched and found me. Since I worked a lot with sexual abuse trauma, he thought I was just the person to help her. If we could just fix *her,* everything would be fine; in fact, his whole life would be pretty darn copacetic. He was not overtly arrogant, just blithely unaware of how blaming he was. He would have been happy to tell me Stella's story and his analysis of their relationship woes. As is so often the case with children of neglect, I had to continually interrupt him and say, "Art, tell me about *you*. Talk about *you*." He had the characteristic attitude of "What's to talk about?"

## A HORSE WITH NO NAME: THE DESERT OF NEGLECT

Art was the only child of a depressive, hypochondriacal mother. Since Art was a tiny baby, he described her laughingly as "MIA," whether languishing in her darkened bedroom, lying on the couch, or just dragging around like a zombie. Art's father was not around much and was prone to anger when he was. He was annoyed by the poorly kept house and his endlessly unhappy wife. He had little attention or patience for Art, tried to make the household livable for himself, and was glad for anything Art could do toward that end. It did not occur to him that a little boy might need care and guidance from parents, or from someone. He simply wished for Art to add minimally to his burden or preferably lighten it.

Art learned early that his mother's flaccid attention was utterly impervious to anything he might say or do. He had no impact. If he made waves, he might attract the irritation or ire of his Dad, if he happened to be around. Most likely his mother would not notice or care too much if he did badly or well at school, in sports, or with other kids. Art roamed around essentially untethered. He was free of many restrictions but also perennially bored and disconnected. He watched a lot of TV and, as he got a little older, found refuge in sports and in science.

Like many children of neglect, Art had sparse memory of childhood, or his memory was minimally about people and relationships. He learned very early, without even realizing that he had learned it, both that he had no impact on the arbitrary and unpredictable vicissitudes of others and that the way to get what he needed was to do for himself.

Art became remarkably skilled and efficient at all kinds of things at precocious ages. He shopped and cooked; he operated a washing machine. He found ways to earn money before he was 10. People outside the home were impressed with his resourcefulness and competence rather than seeing that he had needs. Art himself learned to disavow needs he might have from other people. He liked to think of himself as impressively independent, unencumbered, successful, and free. Although he did not get along that well with other kids, he got along. He did well in school and, when he got older, steadily ascended a career ladder in his profession.

Out of Art's childhood experience emerged a two-pillar belief system about relationship life. The two core truisms were as ever-present as ambient air, so self-evident he did not even need to acknowledge or know them consciously. "I will never get what I need in relationship." And "There is nothing I can do." So the guiding principles of his life in relationship were to do it all himself and to resign himself to having no impact.

## OWNER OF A LONELY HEART: INTIMATE PARTNERSHIP

Although Art's strategy of doing it all himself is practicable in many if not most areas of life, sexuality presents another kind of challenge. It is true we *can* do it all ourselves (as Woody Allen is quick to remind us), but it is not the same. Blessed or cursed with a healthy sexual drive, Art made his best effort at dating and had a number of relationships, although it was hard to make them last. There were lengthy "dry spells" between them, where Art pursued an active solitary sex life and became proficient at taking care of his own needs. He also discovered that going to professionals was sometimes easier for him than trying to make a go of intimacy, although that usually left him feeling empty and ashamed.

When he met Stella, he thought he had found someone different. She seemed to have depth and liveliness; she seemed to see and appreciate his special qualities; she seemed receptive to his brilliance. They did things together, and she even seemed interested in knowing him. Art did not even recognize how being/feeling truly known had been a missing experience for him. It rather dazzled him. In the beginning, the relationship with Stella seemed so promising. It was different and fun. They had sex then, too. It was not chandelier sex, but it was good enough and she seemed to really like him. What went wrong?

## BURNING DOWN THE HOUSE: WHO'S RESPONSIBLE FOR RESENTMENT?

Being with Stella seemed to Art to bring out the best in him. He unleashed his competence and its accompanying generosity in the relationship. He could not do enough for her. It was a new and dizzying experience for him to take care of another person. He had not realized just how good at things he was. It was exciting to see something begin to grow between himself and another person; to see himself reflected in the eyes of another; to see a smile come over Stella's face in response to him. Of course we now know that the early stages of relationship are chemically enhanced with the rich brew of endogenous opioids and PEA. He was intoxicated. And during this time of intoxication he was actively saying yes to her and giving to her with abandon. There was no limit to what he had to offer her.

As the drug high of romantic love began to wane, as it does for all humans, Art began to revert to more familiar ways of being. He thought more as an individual and expressed himself more in first person singular terms than as "we"; he unwittingly was more actively self-reliant and less thoughtful of Stella, certainly less receptive to anything remotely resembling needing her. He was busy and more focused on his work and his own endeavors. This could activate Stella's age-old belief that she was only good for one thing, just as it had been with her stepfather. She began to tense up and have trauma symptoms around sex.

As was his habit, Art continued to say "yes" to what Stella wanted or needed, even when she did not ask. He did not notice that he was agreeing or even offering to take care of household tasks, help her with her computer gaffes, drive her places when she was tired, and pay for things. Before he knew it, Art was doing "everything." It was OK, though, really, because he could, and he was practiced at not expecting or needing anything from anyone. But when the sex started to go off track, a head of steam began to rise in Art. Little by little he was first simmering and then seething with resentment. He wasn't asking for much, after all, and even that was too much. He began to drop into a deep well of childhood anger at being left alone with his needs and having to do and do and do for himself and also for his invalid mother. He was not entirely aware of the part that was from the past. He was just aware that he was increasingly bitter and angry with Stella. He was impatient and often sharp with her and began to experience her as lethargic, depressed, and depressing. He was bored, unenthusiastic about coming home to her, and stayed later and later at work.

However, Art continued to do more than his purported share around the house and cover most of the expenses. He listened to Stella talk about her problems at work or with her family, and increasingly he begrudged her his "generosity" and felt more fiercely entitled to sex when he wanted it. Was that so much to ask? As he got madder and madder, more and more stingingly resentful, he seemed to walk around the house as if in road rage. Stella complained that he was a grouch or worse: that he scared her and reminded her of her brutally threatening stepdad. Hearing that incensed Art, and he felt more bitter, unappreciated, and taken for granted. He felt like a sugar daddy, except he was not getting even a sugar daddy's due.

And why did Art continue to keep doing it all and keep paying for it all, only to resent Stella more? His childhood had trained and bred him to do it all and to endure. His childhood had prepared him and groomed him to live without reciprocity. Only now was he starting to feel the rage of a lifetime about it.

I had to teach Art, "When you overgive and then resent it, it is on you. You are responsible for your own resentment. You need to catch and regulate yourself at the point of the 'yes' to keep yourself out of this trap of rage." Creating indebtedness was not going to get him what he wanted. Quite the opposite. Stella routinely complained, "It's not safe to accept anything from you," which only made him more angry.

## I NEED A LOVER WHO WON'T DRIVE ME CRAZY! FOCUS ON THE OTHER

Growing up with his mother, Art was accustomed to having no impact at all on what would transpire between them. He learned from experience to take that as an unalterable given, and he felt completely and utterly powerless over their interactions and their relationship. He had no choice but to watch and wait. He generally studied her closely, trying to keep himself at least minimally apprised of what was going on. With Stella he did the same. He watched her studiously, then started reading books about trauma and abuse and became the self-styled expert on Stella, sometimes truly believing he understood her better than she understood herself.

Convinced their growing unhappiness was all her fault, Art believed he knew what was required to "fix" her. He began to lecture and harangue her about how "unhealthy" she was and what she "should" be doing about it. Of course she did not take warmly to his amateur (and certainly not neutral!) psychoanalysis of her and was neither inspired to follow his barbed advice, nor inspired toward eroticism or affection. It may have rustled up some guilt or heightened her fear (hardly an aphrodisiac!). That made him angrier still. And the more he waxed self-righteously superior and focused on her, the more weed-entangled and pest-infested became his own "yard."

## DUST IN THE WIND: PASSIVITY

Steeped in the belief that he has no impact, that he is powerless and there is nothing he can do, the child of neglect collapses or freezes. The signature of neglect is passivity. Even an overachiever in other areas of his life like Art, in the throes of relationship turmoil, collapses into inaction. Admittedly, he thought vengefully about having an affair; he thought spitefully about leaving her; he even had horrifying fantasies about things he'd like to say or do to Stella. But characteristically (and fortunately), it was all thought. Even as he punctiliously performed his role, reciting his echoing lines in their seemingly unending battle about sex, Art could feel impotent and believe, "I didn't do anything! There is nothing I *can* do!"

My steadfast conviction that the problem is a 50–50 deal was a hard sell with Art, as it often is with survivors of neglect. Accustomed to the other having all the power and therefore responsibility for the mess, it was a foreign notion that there was in fact decisive action that he was in a position to take and was capable of, not only on his own behalf but even that could affect the course of relationship.

## I WANT YOU TO WANT ME: GETTING TO NEED

It took time and humility for Art to acknowledge that it was not only that he wanted Stella to get "cured" and "put out." His crushing childhood trauma was the chronic experience of being unwanted or rejected. So steeped was he in that experience that he was largely unaware of it. It was just a fact of life. No wonder each time Stella declined his invitation to be intimate with him, it hit him like bricks. Even all of his expertise about sexual abuse and PTSD could not buffer his deeply visceral vulnerability, could not put a dent in his taking her lack of sexual desire for him devastatingly personally.

Art also had little awareness of the impact of his carefully constructed childhood strategy of "not needing anything in relationship." First of all, it was not true. He craved attention and time from Stella. He just wanted her around. He admitted that just having her nearby knitting or banging on the computer in the same room where he was sitting was a comfort to him. He wanted her to want to do things with him and make time to go places with him. He did want to be remembered and he wanted to be touched. It was very difficult for him to express this and to express it gently. He was so defended against rejection that to him it bordered on suicidal to let it be known. And of course he was hard pressed to acknowledge or appreciate what he did get. It seemed dangerous to "let the good stuff in," to let it matter, and to ever reveal that it mattered.

Art preferred to believe the problem was sexual and the sexual problem was Stella's. He balked at the notion that the sexual impasse is 50–50. "I don't have a sex problem and I never have!" he haughtily retorted.

The good news is that if it is all the other person's pathology, the signature refrain of the child of neglect, "There is nothing I can do!" will be true. Art discovered, "If I own half the problem, there *is* in fact a ton that I *can* do. In effect I am empowered to be part of the solution!" It took a fair amount of work for him to view clearly his own developmental trauma—the trauma of attachment—and the flower beds that were his own to landscape, plow, plant, tend, and ultimately harvest.

# Chapter Fifteen

## TANGLED UP IN BLUE: COMMON TRAUMA/ NEGLECT SEXUAL DYNAMICS

What I have come to call the "sexual impasse" braids the many ragged threads of disparate information we have studied in all the previous chapters into one thick, integrated rope. This rope can choke the life out of your relationship, or we can fashion of it a lifeline to pull yourselves out of the mire. We now know that trauma is very much about fragmentation and the shattering apart of the many components of experience. Often memory is chaotic and incomplete. Snippets of visual imagery may not seem to connect to anything, powerful body sensations may seem to come from nowhere, emotions flood forth at devastating random, and behavior seems incomprehensibly beyond control, to have a force of its own. Neglect is about lost threads, gaps in experience, discontinuities, patchy or missing memory, and being invisible and unknown, perhaps even to oneself.

By now we have a pretty clear sense about the tangle of triggering and reactivity. We know that the suffering and the damage in the relationship are from the ricocheting *interplay* between trigger and reaction, stimulus and ignited response. Unless we have both, there is no drama. Again, this is good news and bad. The bad news is that nobody is off the hook. Both partners have work to do to find the way home. The good news is that at any given time, it is fully within the power of one partner to divert an explosion or even spearhead a healing jag simply by attending to his or her own yard. *If one of you fails to react, the volley will hit the wall, sputter, and fade out.* This is a powerful position that is available to either of you.

Perhaps this chapter should come with a warning label. We examine some common trauma/neglect sexual patterns that admittedly may seem painfully bleak. Making sense of all the strands, teasing out meaning, and discovering how they all map together is the arduous work of healing. Both partners, while deconstructing their tattered shared dynamics, are simultaneously reconstructing their individual stories while reconstituting their shared story. No wonder you are exhausted!

I've already described what I refer to as the Grand Collusion. This is where, either explicitly or implicitly, both partners view the designated traumatized person as the problem child. The child of neglect is the designated endurer or saint. These are dangerously easy roles to slide into. Generally, traumatized people are inclined toward guilt and shame, believing they brought their overwhelming experience on themselves or deserved it, or are mercilessly blamed for their woes. And neglect survivors, focused on the all-powerful other, tend to believe they have no impact in relationship because they scarcely exist. Now we begin to delve into the sexual problem. In the Grand Collusion view, the sexual problem belongs to the traumatized person and roles may be sticky and difficult to relinquish. Fasten your seatbelts as we visit a sample of struggling couples. All of them did stay the course and come out the other side.

## HOW DID WE GET HERE? THE MAKING OF THE SEXUAL IMPASSE

When I first met Rob and Elise, Rob lamented, "Remember that song 'Once in a Lifetime' by Talking Heads, where the singer wakes up in a beautiful house, with a beautiful wife, and has no idea how he got there?" Rob was a rock and roll lover and a lively guy. He never imagined himself in a relationship with an attractive and sexy partner whom he loved having no sex at all. It had been going on for over a year now, and he was baffled, bewildered, and fed up.

In the early days of the relationship, Rob remembered having a pretty good time. Although their sex was not imaginative or particularly varied, it was plentiful and fun enough. As he and Elise spent more and more time together, he could pretty much count on having sex every day if he wanted to. He'd always had a strong libido, so that suited him. Or, as he said, "I could get used to that!"

After a certain point, Elise began to cool a bit. Some of it had to do with the wearing off of the first blush of romance and the accompanying endogenous aphrodisiac chemicals. Her natural baseline libido was lower than Rob's. But more, she wanted to do things together. It seemed to her that Rob wanted to spend a "disproportional" amount of their time in bed. She wanted to talk more, to be more active and outdoors together, to share more in other ways.

At first, when Elise declined Rob's erotic overtures, he was surprised and disappointed. He felt hurt and rejected. She said she was tired, that the stress from her job was wearing on her. It was hard for him to believe or accept that. An only child of a single mom, Rob remembered how his mother got swept up in her work. He would fall by the wayside as everything else seemed to take precedence over him. The days were long and empty for him as a boy. He learned early both to entertain himself and to take care of himself. Although he was self-contained and self-sufficient, he was an angrier child than he knew. He was not quite aware just how much it bothered him that his mother was so absent or that she knew so little of his life. He just knew he was bored, perhaps listless, and looked forward to growing up and getting away from home. Elise being busier and less available or less inclined to be intimate with him awakened an old gnawing irritability that he was not fully aware of. He was really getting sick of it.

Elise loved Rob. When they met she was delighted. Relationship had never been easy for her. He seemed to be kind and patient, as well as having a slightly "bad boy" character that she'd always found appealing. It was exciting getting involved with him at first. He seemed to be genuinely interested in her. But after a while she became mildly alarmed. She was not immediately fully aware of it. It just seemed that she and Rob spent an awful lot of their time having sex. Was that all she was good for? Did he really even care about her for anything else? She became suspicious and perhaps annoyed by the emphasis on sex. She wanted to be valued for who she was. Of course when she spoke of this to Rob, he was incensed and insulted. Implied was that she both viewed him as a sex-obsessed brute and failed to see all the other ways he showed her his love. At least, that was how he heard it.

Rob's anger scared Elise and also made her feel all the more that he just didn't get it or he didn't get her, which made her feel that much less amorous. Elise's sexual abuse by her stepfather began when she was 8. Her parents' divorce had been an ugly one and when her mother brought her stepfather into the family, he seemed genuinely fond of her. He seemed to initiate time with her and took her places in a way that made her feel special, which she had never felt with her dad. The sexual abuse confused her, and as she grew older she came to believe that she would only ever be valued for sex. She had no other worth. At first she had felt that Rob was different. Now he was turning out to be the same as all the other men in her life who had either left or used her.

Elise's stepdad was prone to rages and controlled the household with angry threats or fiery outbursts. She had made a lifelong effort to stay clear of angry men as much as she was able. Rob had seemed to her to be so even tempered. The rigidly patterned collision course began to take shape. It could begin with either partner. Rob might attempt a sexual invitation or innuendo; Elise might deflect it, respond less than enthusiastically, or even wordlessly tense up. Rob would be first hurt or disappointed, then irritation or anger might show on his face. Even without words, Elise might sense anger, anticipating retaliation. She would withdraw, maybe subtly, maybe overtly. Rob, violently sensitive to withdrawal, would then become more obviously angry. Elise then would decisively withdraw, perhaps going to another room to sleep or leaving the house.

Elise started coming home later and later from work. She dreaded the conflict between them, so she attempted to avoid it however she could. When there were business trips to be taken, she readily volunteered; when there were work projects that spilled over into the weekends, she was generous with her help. At least at work she felt valued for something. Rob's anger became increasingly distasteful as well as scary to her. She wondered if she was losing her love for him.

When they found their way to therapy, Rob and Elise had been cycling and sucked loudly downward like old bathwater down the drain for some time. Like many couples, they'd let it go on until both were thin on hope and heavy on blame. When "I don't matter" meets "I'll never get what I need in relationship," the mighty confluence can build momentum to the magnitude of flash floods.

## NO MORE "BAD LOVE": ON BEING DESIRED

Sandy was exasperated and worn out by another painful and demoralizing, looping interaction. Although Jan was willing to have sex, it seemed to be on the order of obligatory or "mercy" sex. Sandy felt no heat of passion coming from Jan, no electricity, or to use Sandy's words, "not a whiff of feeling wanted." Sex felt mechanical, flat, and ultimately lonely. "Is it too much to ask for a tiny spark?" Apparently it was. The barrenness of the sexual exchange seemed to replicate Sandy's vacuous and empty childhood, devoid of touch, play, laughter, and connection. Not necessarily conscious of the painful triggered connection to childhood, Sandy was simply aware that sex with Jan had become unbearable. "It was a kind of agony! I felt ashamed and humiliated to continue to want someone who did not want me!" Hurt and furious, Sandy just shut down sexually and stopped trying. "No sex is better than bad sex! And I knew hell could freeze over before Jan would ever want sex with me!"

The research on avoidant attachment describes mothers who are repelled by their infants' bodies. The baby, at a body level, might experience a devastating physical rejection long before having the cognitive equipment or language to "know" it. The infant might subsist with a kind of "skin hunger" that as the child grows older may not make sense. We know that for the very young, physical contact is the essence of communication as well as being a source of comfort and reassurance. Of course, we could not know what Sandy's infancy was like, but as an older child, the memory of a cold and distant family life was unquestionable and persistent. The longing to be physically wanted was deep in Sandy's body, as were the hurt and anger about not receiving it. The sexual shutdown happened wordlessly, although the air grew thick with tension and sarcasm.

For Jan it was frightening. "Sandy turned into someone I did not know."

Jan's trauma was sexual. From one day to the next, something strange and awful began happening. "I was 12 and my big brother was 17. I had always looked up to him. Suddenly without warning, he turned into a monster who did things to me and did not care about my feelings at all. I was so shocked and blindsided, as well as confused and hurt. He never said anything to me. He just changed. It was like night and day." Jan was just barely entering puberty when the abuse began, and sex never did grow into something positive or enjoyable. "I rarely talked about what happened with my brother. I just didn't ever want to have much sex. I did tell Sandy, although I wasn't sure it was important. And no, I never thought of going to therapy until Sandy started nagging me nonstop to go. That sure didn't make me want to go!"

Jan admitted that not having sex was a relief in a way. The momentary respite, however, was more than outweighed by the traumatic trigger of Sandy "turning into someone else that I did not really know." That was terrifying, as was the cyclone of anger and withdrawal that became the climate of their household.

## LOVE STINKS!: GIVING AND RECEIVING

Fred's neglect was severe. And his feeling like a stepchild was compounded by the fact that his sister was the "golden child." With excruciating precision, he watched as she got all sorts of advantages and privilege that he did not get. He did not know if it had to do with her being a girl or if there was something special about her that he just did not have. But he was bitter and envious and became preoccupied with questions of equality and justice and who got what. Fred learned to expect to get nothing, although he never got used to it.

Fred was smart, and he grew to be exquisitely capable and apt at taking care of himself. As he got older and had relationships outside his family, Fred's expectation persisted that he could not hope to get anything he needed. He certainly did not feel entitled to ask. As time went on, however, he developed a brilliantly resourceful strategy. He may not even have been fully aware of it. By giving copiously to others, he "earned" the right to reciprocity. After all, "fair is fair." It was his own self-protective remake of the "pay it forward" concept. By giving first, he secured entitlement to call in his debt.

Rosa shrank from contact with Fred. She never seemed to be able to gain any ground. Her efforts at being loving never seemed to count. On the contrary, most of what she heard from Fred was criticism and complaint about how unloving and ungiving she was. She was so tired of hearing it that she could explode, which she often did, with bouts of rageful yelling followed by torrential tears and silence.

Rosa's trauma was relentless emotional abuse where she was repeatedly and viciously taunted and criticized for falling short in every way. She was too fat, too slow, too messy, too chaotic, the list was endless. Hers was an angry family, where voices were raised and people talked over each other or shouted to be heard. Rosa had frayed self-esteem, of course. She longed to feel loved, and both in and outside her family she worked hard to please. She was bright and did well in school, so although relationships were painfully challenging, she succeeded in building a successful career. When she met Fred, she hoped that it would be different. He was older and seemed to think well of her, at least at the beginning.

Sex virtually stopped long before I met Fred and Rosa. Both were deeply embittered. Rosa was devastated by Fred's life paradigm in which love was such a "calculated and mercenary exchange of services." She wanted to live in a world where love was freely given, where she would be loved based on affection and connection, not accounts payable. She felt beholden all the time and it choked and stifled her loving feelings and broke her heart.

Fred felt profoundly unloved living in a sexless marriage. He also felt colossally shortchanged. "I agreed to monogamy, not the Sahara desert!" He felt not only deeply hurt by being unwanted but also betrayed and cheated and denied a basic human need. His criticism was pointedly logical, and he seemed to keep a running tally of what he did for Rosa that she never seemed to want to repay. It echoed the chronic resounding reprimand pounding like a raucous bass backbeat off the walls of her childhood home. Fred was heartbroken also, as the young boy must have been who watched his sister showered with all the goodies that he craved. It broke my heart to watch the two of them in their desperate attempts to shield themselves from each other's blows while feeling so bereft.

Round and round. Rosa yelled to try and get love and Fred criticized to try and get sex, both haunted by childhood memories of staccato yelling and both with a deep yearning for something different, hoping and afraid to hope that they might find a way to make it work.

## WE GOTTA GET OUT OF THIS PLACE: GETTING OFF THE MERRY-GO-ROUND

Of course, this is not an exhaustive exposition of all the possible variations on the trauma–neglect interplay. But you get the idea. All these couples had a few vital principles that enabled them to chart their course. Here is the essential take-home message for them as for you:

1. The sexual impasse is not really about sex, or certainly not only about sex, but about myriad other things, too. And by impasse, I do not necessarily mean that sex has stopped completely. But relaxed, connecting, loving sex is what is stalled.

2. The problem is dynamic, meaning it is a "social product," cocreated by the *interaction* of components that hail from both partners.
3. It spans the widest spectrum of human experience: body, emotion, belief, behavior, relationship, past, present, and future. So we have both many rivers to cross and many possible approaches.
4. Although many partners come in earnestly and honestly wishing to just get the *other* partner "fixed," once and for all, I'm afraid it does not work that way.

All that being said, I am infinitely optimistic and hopeful. With two willing partners, a profound healing can be achieved. As I often say, "You just can't imagine what you can't imagine." So now, on to Part IV.

# Part IV

# PRACTICE

## Chapter Sixteen

# THE WAY IT IS: ASSESSMENT

Now, after laboring through a lot of dense information, we are approaching the action part of our journey. It is as if we are moving through the security checkpoint at the airport before we head for the gate to board the plane. A few final reminders as we make our way. First, the Decade of the Brain brought us the dramatic discovery that the brain is plastic throughout the lifespan. What this means is that experience changes the brain both in creating new synapses or connections and also in terms of generating new neurons. We used to believe that after the brain reached full development in late adolescence, it was a downhill slide thereafter and that our finite supply of brain cells slowly died off, leaving us increasingly feebleminded with age. We now know that that is not true! Neurogenesis, the birth and growth of new neurons, can continue as long as we continue to breathe.

There are three key leavening agents for neurogenesis: novelty, enriched environments, and physical exercise. (I like to say that with good sex, we get all three!) New and expansive experiences, endeavors, and environments that expose us to challenges and learning spawn fresh brain growth. We know from attachment research that the brain develops and grows in resonance, that the symphonic interplay between infants' and caregivers' brains shapes the growing child's biochemistry and neuroanatomy. The radical new information is that the powerful rhythmic catalyst is mutual. The infant is both created by and creates the parents.

This is also profoundly significant for our purposes. Our mutual experiences with our partners also have the potential to be brain changing. Just as the continued triggering and retraumatization that unhealed partners inflict on each other can more deeply groove the traumatic brain circuitry and in effect make both partners' trauma worse, so in turn do we have the possibility of engendering new healing circuits and brain growth in our partners and of course ourselves. Creating novelty and movement that combines powerful emotional, sensory, relational, and meaning-making components makes of the sexual healing endeavor a potent metamorphic elixir. I find this phenomenally exciting. It also invests us with a serious and consequential mission. Believe it or not, you are unquestionably a very important person in your partner's life. What we are doing is as monumental as brain surgery. And it can extend lifelong.

Attachment research gives us another important piece of information to take along. In the best-case scenario of secure attachment, the percentage of time that infant and caregiver are in attuned harmonic resonance is 30 percent! That is the best case! What this means is that secure attachment, optimal relatedness, is an endless pendular swing between connection, rupture, and repair, back again, and again and again. The brain in relationship is flexible and forgiving: It missteps, corrects, and keeps on going if the repair is prompt and thoroughgoing. Sadly, children of trauma and neglect live in an impoverished relational world, largely devoid of any repair at all. Repair skills, for the most part unknown to these children and later adults, are what make for a safe world and relationships that are sustainable through time. Developing these repair skills changes everything. Repair skills mean that the human inevitability of making mistakes is hardly fatal! What a relief!

Pack these two essential notions with you as we go forward: neurogenesis, the care and feeding of your and your partners' brains; and the crucially significant (and certainly associated) functions of relationship repair.

## WATCHING THE WHEELS GO ROUND AND ROUND: IDENTIFYING OUR PATTERNS

When I first meet a couple, of course I want to hear what brings them and how they characterize their problem. I ask each partner respectively because more often than not, each of them describes the state of the union (or disunion) completely differently. I take as given that there will be at least two versions of their story. Most couples, by the time they reach my door, have been struggling for some time and most likely pondering or even obsessing about their anguished daily life, which to them feels like a chaotic battle zone. To them it seems as if bombs randomly fall and they constantly stumble over and trip explosive hidden land mines. What I try to help them to see is that generally speaking, there is a redundant cycling, patterned interaction repeating again and again—like an old scratched vinyl record, for those of us old enough to remember those. The words to the old songs, the content of the conflicts may vary, but it is the same tired fight, over and over. The good news is that once we identify the skeleton of the pattern and the core elements, we find they are few. And our work is cut out for us.

As I listen to this new couple, I will quietly attempt to suss out their attachment styles. In the first moments of my initial meeting with Alex and Robin, I got a vivid preview. Robin, frantic and wordy, ranted at breakneck speed before I even had a chance to set up the framework for our conversation. Alex's flooded reaction was to quietly "check out," almost sleepily withdrawing energy and attention. Robin, immediately sensing Alex's withdrawal, became nearly hysterical, collapsing into heaving sobs and barely able to convey to me that this is what Alex "always" does during any attempt at talking about the relationship. Alex's facial reaction to Robin's emotional display looked like bored annoyance, as if to say, "Here we go again . . . "

Even before knowing the relationship story and the trauma/neglect back story, I could see that Alex was probably an "avoidant" in the language of attachment styles, surviving in a quiet barricaded internal cave. Robin was probably an "anxious ambivalent" going into a state of emergency at the first whiff of "abandonment." I was able to simply name it: Alex, crowded out by a flood of words, feeling "As ever, it is all about you," retreats into the relative safety of solitude. Robin, panicked by the retreat, becomes louder and rapidly dissolves into inconsolable protest. Far from being chaotic, this is a classic scene not only from their life but also from the annals of attachment theory.

Naming and making sense out of the reactions of both from an attachment standpoint made a momentary dent in each of their beliefs that one or both of them was truly crazy. Because they were the parents of their own infant, they were readily able to visualize a baby being either dismissed and left alone or waiting too long in distress for an unreliable, erratic caregiver. With just a little bit of structure, we can transform an unwieldy, intense forum for discussion into a relatively ordered one. Going back to Chapter 1 on attachment styles, can you identify your attachment style? What about your partner? How can you tell?

## SHELTER FROM THE STORM: PRIMARY DEFENSE MECHANISMS

The nature of human survival is to somehow adapt. Even in dramatic, life-threatening circumstances like a concentration camp, the human organism searches out and ultimately creates a default mode of enduring the untenable. The resourcefulness of the brain and body and the spirit, too, may be quite remarkable. However, that default survival mode often persists far beyond the danger that engendered it. What began as a brilliant lifesaving strategy might outlive its usefulness to become a nuisance or worse.

A dramatic example of such an adaptation is Louise, whose trauma, beginning when she was only 4, was so brutal and extreme that while it was happening she just "went away." She might have floated up to the ceiling and looked down at "another little girl" being violently abused on the bed below, or sometimes she just "blanked out" and went unconscious. The memory of her abuse was sealed off into a cavernous compartmentalized hiding place in her psyche. But as an adult, when her partner approached her for sex, the terrorized little girl was suddenly back, and her baffled and bewildered partner was faced with a very large "4-year-old." Obviously what had served Louise as a means of survival in her horrific childhood wrought confusion and havoc in her adult sexual life.

Louise suffered from a severe dissociative disorder, which is one adaptation to trauma wherein experience is split into distinctly separate vault-like compartments. This was the primary defense that sustained her through the horrors of her early life. Not everyone has such dramatic defenses. Alex's defense against a neglectful parent who wielded all the power in the relationship and took up all the space was to shut down and make others unimportant, essentially disavowing need. Robin's defense against being forgotten or left was to shriek louder and to create a ruckus or even an emergency that could not be ignored. Long after leaving the home where these defensive modes were life sustaining, the habit of resorting to them under stress or when current stimuli resembled the original stressors was an unconscious default. Of course, the activated defense mechanisms are potent dance steps in the looping choreography of adult relational dynamics. So it is essential to "update the files" to attend to present time relationship. The clearest way to uncover lingering primary defensive strategies is through identifying core wounds.

## TORN AND FRAYED: CHILDHOOD WOUNDS

By "childhood wounds," we mean the aspects of childhood that were most distressing. Regrettably, everyone has something. Often the child of neglect has little memory or is convinced that "nothing happened to me," which may be quite true given that with neglect, much of the trauma is about *missing* experience; the trauma is in fact that *nothing* happened when there is much that *should have* happened. Again, by identifying core wounds, we are not out to bash parents! This is a decidedly no-blame paradigm! We are not looking to blame parents, perpetrators, or anyone else. We are looking to make sense out of current experience to both inspire empathy and change unwanted behavior.

Andy was offended by my characterization that he was a child of neglect. He considered that an insult to his hard working, self-sacrificing single mother. Andy's father had died when Andy was 7, leaving his mom with three little ones. His mother was so grief stricken that rather than dealing with his own loss, Andy just attempted to take up whatever slack he could and not make any demands on anyone. Andy, being the oldest, was in the position to help his mother with the other kids and to be the little "man of the house." He was shopping and cooking when he was 9 and earning money when he was barely 11. His mother worked two jobs and he was largely on his own virtually from the time of his father's death. Andy admired his mother, and he was proud of his resourcefulness and his independence. He got a lot done, he taught himself to do many things, and he was helpful.

It was not immediately obvious to Andy that being busy and productive and disavowing any need of other people were enduring defensive strategies. Andy's partner, however, felt worthless, unimportant, and not received, lamenting, "Nothing I have to offer is of any value to you! Well, except one thing!" And the kind of intimacy that comes of interdependence and vulnerability was not an option for Andy.

We are best able to locate and name core childhood wounds by examining our current reactivity. What stimuli most readily elicit an overreaction or a reaction disproportional to the stimulus? For Charlotte, unanticipated surprises evoked a storm of rage. Her childhood was peppered with dramatic, lengthy abandonments and random beatings erupting without warning, out of left field. Fred, you will remember, was incensed by inequality and what he perceived as others receiving preferential treatment. He bristled uncontrollably about double standards or Rosa not doing her share.

Most survivors of childhood trauma and neglect have had some measure of individual therapy to process their childhoods, some quite a bit. They may have done so much work already that they are humiliated and shocked by how activated they get. They might very well be tempted to blame their partners for this, proclaiming, "I don't have these problems with anybody else!" Or "My friends say . . ."

Fortunately and unfortunately, the intimate partnership takes us to deeper places in ourselves than anything else I know of. One of the reasons I began doing couples work with trauma survivors was that the work seemed to be more profound, more direct, and quicker than any other work I had done around trauma. No relationship is more family-like, emotionally, physically, and in terms of basic "dailyness," than the intimate and sexual bond. Of course, nothing is as difficult, either. I make no bones about it: This is the hardest thing you'll ever do and the most worth it.

What is your core injury? Can you describe it to your partner? What was your childhood adaptation/reaction to it? Can you tell your partner any stories about that? How do you see the shadow of your core wound and adaptation in your character? How do you perceive the reverberations for your old primary defense in your current life and in your life with your partner? You will most likely discover that your half of the sexual conundrum is another expression of this. But I am getting ahead of myself!

## YOU SAY GOODBYE AND I SAY HELLO:
## CORE RELATIONSHIP DYNAMICS

Alex and Robin unveiled their core relationship dynamic within the first minutes of our initial session. Highly economical time use, I must say! With most couples, it does not take long at all before I get to see their core dynamic. Of course, it is harder to see clearly when you are in it yourselves. Most likely you are most aware of the ways that your partner is "overreacting" and "unreasonable." It might be harder to observe your own reactivity or to see through the content to the process that we keep looping around the same tired old track. We may be tempted to believe that because it is sometimes about who does the dishes, sometimes about lateness, and sometimes about sex, it is not the same pattern.

As we know from Chapter 6, in the moment of trauma and in moments of triggered trauma activation, the logical, reasoning part of the brain is offline. So when you are activated, you are not thinking with your cognitively able brain. And by definition, when you and your partner are having an episode, you are both triggered, so there is no clear-thinking adult brain present in that moment. That is one good reason for couples therapy for trauma/neglect couples. In order to begin to identify and process the core injuries and the core interactions between them, for partners to have one person in the room who is not in trauma activation and who may make the essential difference between progress and stagnation.

Again, the core dynamic is the interplay we have seen over and over again between reaction and reaction. One partner's trauma is activated and the incumbent trauma reaction is precisely what activates the trauma of the other partner, who then reacts with precisely what exacerbates the trauma of the originally triggered partner, and it goes higher, and the other partner's reaction goes higher, etcetera, etcetera, etcetera. By now we have seen enough examples that you know what I mean.

If you are able, ponder your childhood and see if you can name your core wound and primary defense. Reflect on the worst episodes of conflict with your partner. Can you discern the outline or vestige of your core childhood wound embedded in the reaction to your partner? Think about it individually at first. It takes honesty and humility to look at yourself in this way. Only then discuss this with your partner.

Make your best effort at staying in your own yard! It is tempting to psycho-analyze your partner! You may be a highly skilled amateur or even professional psychotherapist. Trust me, your partner will probably not appreciate your brilliant (and possibly quite accurately insightful) offer of free therapy. It may very well spur another activation. But if you are able to use your analytic and intuitive talent to look at yourself and share *that* with your partner, you might get an empathic and appreciative response that will advance our cause and help begin to disarm the dynamic between you.

## SHINE A LIGHT: WHERE ARE WE NOW?

Before we go on to the more overtly sexual terrain, we want to have a clear assessment. Ask yourselves the following questions:

1. Do you know your *attachment style* and your partner's? Do you see vulnerabilities in the relationship stemming from attachment style? Might there be ways you can help each other with those vulnerabilities?
2. Can you name your *core wound*? Are you and your partner able to have the conversation where you each name your own, even acknowledging how they show themselves in your relationship with each other? Are you able to stay in your own yard and talk about yourself?
3. Can you see your *primary defense* strategy? How does that play out in the relationship? Are you able to talk about that with each other? This reflects a lot of ownership and humility. Gentleness in your responses to each other about this demonstrates compassion and care.
4. Can you locate and describe your problematic *core dynamic*, the interplay between your respective core injuries and defense strategies? If you can do all this, you have journeyed a great distance. Working with the core dynamic once it is identified is challenging. However, knowing what it is, accepting that it is a 50–50 undertaking, and being willing to work with it represents a *huge* step.
5. Finally, have a look in your toolbox. How is your *communication*? How are you doing at expressing yourselves and hearing each other with an outcome of understanding? Empathy? Can you talk and listen without getting triggered a good percentage of the time? How is your general level of *connection*? How are your *repair skills*? Can you get back together fairly readily after a disconnection?

Answer these questions for yourself and discuss your answers with your partner. Your answers will help determine if we are ready to start edging toward the bedroom.

## Chapter Seventeen

# HUMAN TOUCH: BEING HERE NOW

"It hurts," Anna lamented, "when Larry touches me it hurts. He's not doing anything wrong . . ." "Yeah," Larry chimed in. "Then she cringes and shrinks away. It's all over." Anna continued, "In a heartbeat he pulls away, rolls over and goes to sleep. I lie there for hours wide-eyed. I hate myself. I'm a bad person . . . But I can't help it . . ." "That's OK," Larry retorted in a sharp staccato that belied his words. "I'm done trying." Anna's only response to this was her anguished face and collapsed body. It was as if they were calling the steps to a tired, old square dance that was no fun at all.

Anna grew up in a violent alcoholic home where the only touch she knew was abusive. She was hit with belts, wooden spoons, hairbrushes, fists, and open hands. Virtually anything would do. The blows were unpredictable, seemingly random. She learned to sustain a posture of high alert: vigilant attention and a body poised to flee. Young Anna was on edge even when in bed, often rudely awakened by the slamming and yelling of her parents' drunken fights. Being flooded with adrenalin, muscles tight as a drum, was Anna's baseline state when she was at home. Like ambient air, she no longer even noticed it.

In junior high Anna became a cross-country runner, so her wiry physique and agility at flight became assets, and no one knew what was going on inside of her. Running long distance enabled her to open some miles between herself and that battle zone. The havoc never abated until one day without warning her parents announced their decision to divorce and dumped her off to live with relatives in another city. Although the relatives were cool and disinterested, they were not mean, so Anna's high school years were somewhat quieter. By then, however, hyperarousal and tension, like a coiled spring, were her default mode, and unpredictability was her nemesis.

Larry had little to say about his background. He described his childhood as ordinary and uneventful, nothing unusual had happened. "It was a regular, whitebread upbringing. My father was a doctor, there was plenty of money. My mom was a housewife." It was so unremarkable he hardly remembered it. His memory seemed to begin with college. Larry was much more interested in talking about Anna's childhood and getting help with "Anna's problems."

Only slowly over time did Larry's story take shape. His mother never meant to have a child, never wanted to. She had Larry to placate her husband, Larry laughed when he told us. Larry could not remember how he knew this, but he always had. His mother suffered from depression and frail health his whole life. She was gratified and relieved that Larry was so independent and self-sufficient starting at early ages. Larry was so busy learning how to operate an alarm clock and get his own breakfast that he scarcely noticed how unwanted he was. Granted, there was no hugging in his house, but he was not aware that anything else was missing. He had food, shelter, clothing, and education, so the fact that his mother spent much of her time in bed or watching TV did not seem unusual to him. It was true that he was bored and that no one knew him, but that was hardly abusive from his point of view. Larry graduated early and went to college in a distant city. His father paid for grad school as well. He rarely saw his parents.

## RIGHT HERE RIGHT NOW

Anna and Larry continued describing their dynamic. Over and over again it was the same tedious, miserable dance. "Sometimes I just lie in bed and sob. Larry seems to roll into a tighter, harder ball, curling into himself like a potato bug. Then I feel even more bereft. No sympathy. What kind of person just gets angrier when I'm in pain? What am I doing here? This is just like my lousy family!" Anna's face contorted into angry tears as she spoke. Looking over at Larry, I could see his jaw twitching with tense impatience, even disgust. His eyes looked hard. He said nothing. Clearly he was sick of it. I could imagine the two of them lying in bed, each with a voice shrieking inside, "Make it stop! Make it stop!"

Looking back and forth from one to the other, I said to them, "This is it, isn't it? It's happening right now." Brilliantly, they were unveiling the heart of the battle scene before my eyes as couples often do. "The nature of trauma is to re-enact it," I softly said. "That goes for shock trauma like yours, Anna, and developmental trauma or neglect, like yours Larry." Larry looked annoyed at the implication that he also had trauma.

Because so often the trauma story has no words and does not seem even vaguely to cohere into anything describable, the fractured emotions and body sensations display themselves in behaviors and reactions that often seem to have a life of their own. They persist in replaying themselves until they finally get heard. Then we can make it stop.

Anna remembered being a little girl and feeling like this. She would be scared and hurt, having just been whacked with a wooden spoon. Choking with tears, she would see the hardened face of her mother glaring vacantly at her. Then she felt so alone she wanted to die. That was how she felt when Larry approached her, hurt her, and then withdrew. Why could he not understand this?

Larry looked impatient, as if he were gathering himself up and getting ready to leave my office. Anna had a look of alarm, almost panic. Again I looked from one to the other. Larry looked completely and utterly fed up, Anna frantic to find a way out of this knot so he would not leave, literally or figuratively. I asked Larry, "Does this feel familiar to you? This angry impatience, what does it remind you of?"

"The other five million times we've been through this!" he snapped, looking as if he'd had it with me, too.

"Anything else? From childhood?"

Then Larry surprised us all. His face got a faraway look for a moment and suddenly he seemed to be back. It was as if the blurry colors were slowly sharpening and shaping into the recognizable image in a Polaroid photo. His voice softened. "I do remember something. My mother was so pathetic. Her migraines, her cramps, her ulcers, her 'bad days ...' It was always something. She was always bellyaching about something, and I was supposed to feel sorry for her and help her more. It really got old. I guess I just wanted her to be like other moms who cooked dinner and even slightly remembered that there was someone else there besides herself ... "

Anna looked at Larry, who looked genuinely sad. She was wide-eyed, and her body seemed to be craning, reaching toward him. She could imagine a little boy in a big house with a disheveled, depressed, hypochondriac mother, weighed down by an unhappiness that expanded to occupy all available space in their home and world. Anna's face softened more as Larry perceptibly scavenged deeply inside himself. She noticed her own movement, her urge to reach out to him. He looked genuinely and deeply sad. As Larry slowly emerged from his reverie, he seemed to rejoin us in the room. His face took on first an expression of amazement, and then he looked rather like the cat that had just swallowed a canary. All he said was "Wow!"

When the child of neglect first begins to recoup his or her own history, it is a kind of homecoming. With self-discovery comes emotion and connection with self. It is a kind of reclaiming or coming alive. Anna's face filled with a glowing warmth. "That's the guy I fell in love with."

It was our first chunk of trauma processing. Processing is when the stimulus from present-time reality activates emotion, behavior, and body sensations harkening back to traumatic events. Consciously connecting the dots between stimulus, emotion, sensation, and memory and putting the pieces together coherently in words is integration. This is how things begin to change. Anna and Larry saw how they were suddenly together completely differently. The redundant old dynamic had dissolved and given way to the present moment. Now we could begin to look differently at their dynamic. Even if it did not change and stop happening immediately, now we were on our way. Larry had made a first step into beginning to inhabit himself and, freed from scrutiny and blame, Anna felt infinitely freer and more spacious in her own yard.

Sexuality and touch take place in the present moment. Trauma healing is all about being *here* and not *there*, occupying the present moment instead of living in the past. The lion's share of the work of sexual recovery is this.

## AGAINST THE WIND: COMING HOME TO SENSATION

Now that we had a better idea of what was going on inside of Larry, I turned to Anna. What happened inside when Larry touched her? She knew only that she flinched, cringed, shrank away. That was all she knew. Often afterward, she would barely remember what had happened, just feeling awash with anxiety. It was Larry's angry withdrawal that stirred the emotions of sadness, frustration, and anger, and it was his hardening against her sadness that she most remembered after an episode. So focusing on the touch aspect was difficult for her.

I asked Anna if she was still a runner, knowing that cross-country had been one of her primary modes of self-regulation, one of the most reliable ways she had found as a young person of calming herself down. She said yes, she still ran. I asked her if she was aware of how she felt in her body when she was running, and what she thought about.

Anna looked embarrassed. She had never really talked about this with anyone before, so had never talked about it in front of Larry. She looked away. "For a long time, all I think about is how long until it's over, all I can think about is wanting to stop . . . After I hit about mile 10, I stop thinking about wanting it to be over and start to hit my stride. My mind starts to roam to other things."

"By the end of the run I feel really good and mellow. That is the arc. Of course I dread starting a run because of that long time of just thinking about when it will end. Even if I tell myself that I will feel better, it is hard to stay with it. I have to grind through that dread every single day. That is why I always do the same route, because I know exactly where I am when I start to calm down." Anna looked nervous as she revealed this. I asked her to notice what she was feeling in her body right then. She said she felt tense all over and a rush of adrenalin. Her chest was tight and her stomach was in a knot. This was how she felt when she was out running, and not that different from how she felt sometimes with Larry. I suggested she just let her thoughts go and focus on her body sensations in the moment.

Anxiety is about rushing off into the future. It is uncertain. And there is a feedback loop between thoughts and sensations. Thinking, "I can't wait until this is over, when is this going to be over?" might create unpleasantness when in fact there is no real discomfort or pain happening. The thoughts themselves may activate tension. Making an experiment of setting the thoughts and even the emotions aside for a moment, and just being with her body, Anna watched the tension very quickly drain away. She was actually fine. I said to Anna, "Right here, right now, in this very moment, everything is fine." And it was.

Anna realized that the same thing was happening with Larry's touch. She was in dread before it even began, and when he touched her, she was first startled and then raced ahead with murky, anxious thoughts, like mindless terror. We continued to track her sensations moment to moment in our session. She was amazed to see how readily she calmed down when she did that.

A number of approaches to trauma healing teach the practice of mindful awareness of body sensation moment to moment. In the moment of trauma, it is as if time stands still. In a strange and deathly way, one feels as if the overwhelming experience will never end or as if there is no time. Seeing sensation move and change moment to moment is a visceral experience of time advancing, of progress. Observing change, even subtle sensory change, is somehow reassuring. Life goes on. Feeling pressure lessen, tension release, and relief brings some sense of hope. It also begins to groove an alternative, new circuit in the brain rather than follow the same old one. Anna was heartened to see how much optimism and confidence she gained through this simple practice. It is a powerful and essential conscious skill for our purposes that we will return to again and again.

Larry had opened the door to his story. Anna had awoken to her present-time body sensation. We were on our way.

## DON'T DO ME LIKE THAT! CHOREOGRAPHING NEW PATTERNS

Having begun to discern the deeper layers of the repeating pattern, we set about the task of moving into present time with new ones. As we began to even imagine fashioning something new and uniquely their own, it became clear that Larry and Anna, like so many other couples, had no idea of each other's preferences in terms of touch and sex. Larry rather assumed that Anna did not like anything, and Anna rather assumed that Larry didn't care what she liked and so just did whatever he wanted. Of course, they had never talked about any of this.

Many couples go through their whole lives without ever talking about likes and dislikes about touch and sex. For some the reason is shame. Others believe they are supposed to just know or that there was some instruction manual that was handed out on a day they were absent. Many individuals don't even realize that there may be infinite variations. They just figure, "There is something wrong with you!" or "There is something wrong with me!" I like to begin with the following practice, which is a structured conversation. First of all, it is a foray into a new way to talk about touch and sex.

But first, a word about "practice." You've probably figured out by now that I am a person who loves and cares about words. One thing I discovered early on was that everyone seemed to cringe and recoil from the word *homework*. Too many years of school tainted that word with every imaginable association, most not helpful to our endeavor. *Exercises* seemed to conjure something contrived, artificial, and shallow. It was equally unattractive.

I discovered that I like the word *practice*. I associate it with spiritual life. A spiritual practice is a consistent and deepening active commitment to a particular, chosen kind of life, generally including a component of consciousness, intentionality, and action. A psychotherapy practice for me is my ever-evolving shaping of my work. Sports practice is the organized rehearsal of skills and activities to the end of becoming increasingly adept and proficient. In general, practice is the never-ending embrace of repetition for the purpose of improvement. I like to call our structured activities practices.

---

### PRACTICE #1: THE IDEAL TIME AND PLACE: WHAT ARE THE OPTIMAL CONDITIONS FOR INTIMACY FOR YOU?

There is a time and place for everything, or certainly an optimal time and place. And each of us is different. For intimacy, we have a far better chance of having things go well if partners know each other's idealized scenarios and are able to accommodate each other's preferences to some extent. Many people, as important as this is, have never stopped to really think about their ideal conditions, let alone discussed them with their partners. This activity is intended to facilitate both: to help you think about what your vision might be and then to articulate it to your partner.

Sex Therapist Linda Alperstein suggests that there are four main categories or conditions that we each have our preferences about. These are

1. the physical environment
2. the physical state of yourself
3. the emotional state of yourself
4. the state of the relationship

Take them one by one.

## 1. The Physical Environment

Some people are more discerning than others about their surroundings. What do you prefer in the physical environment for intimacy? You may be more or less particular. You may have never thought about this. Don't let that worry you! You can think as you go, and you may find that you change your mind as time goes on or as you try different things.

- Do you like to be intimate at home or somewhere else? A hotel? Out of doors somewhere?
- Do you prefer the bedroom or somewhere else in the house? The living room rug? The couch? Another room?
- Do you like a warm temperature? Or cool? A fire in the fireplace? The heat on? Windows open or closed?
- What sort of light do you like? Soft or dimmed lights? Candlelight? A well-lit room? Semi-darkness? Pitch darkness?
- Do you like music or silence? What sort of music do you like? Loud or soft?
- What about fragrance? Do you like the scent of flowers or incense? Or do you prefer just plain fresh, clean air?
- Is it important to you to have clean sheets? Or that the room be clean and tidy? Or are you flexible about the state of order in the room?
- Anything else I may have not thought of?

## 2. The Physical State of Yourself

People are very different about this too! Some people would not dream of being sexual when they are not feeling well or when they are menstruating, for example. Others are not deterred by these conditions. Take your time and think about what conditions of your own and your partner's body are most conducive/attractive to you.

- Cleanliness and hygiene: Is it important to you to be very clean, to bathe or shower before you and your partner are close? Do you like a little sweat or find body odor sexy? How clean do you wish your partner to be? Do you feel free to tell your partner?
- Is it important to you that you shave before making close bodily contact? And/or that your partner shave?
- What about fragrances? Do you like cologne or perfume? Some people find them very sexy and appealing. Some are turned off or even allergic.

- When you are tired or ill, does it change your feelings about being close? What about menstruation? Do you feel free to tell you partner honestly? Do you have judgments about illness, your own or your partner's?
- Anything else about the state of your or your partner's body that I may have missed?

## 3. Emotional Condition

For some people, intimacy is difficult when there is worry, upset, or some sort of anxiety. They find it too distracting to focus on being close and in the moment. Others are soothed by the touch and find it comforting and helpful. How is it for you?

- Are you open to being physically intimate if you are worried or upset?
- When you are pressured or stressed or facing a deadline of some sort, does the intimacy feel like a support or an additional source of stress?
- How important is it to you to know that you have plenty of privacy? Are you comfortable with children (or parents or other people) in the house when you are being intimate? Windows open? Curtains?
- Do you need to know there is plenty of time? Do you need to know there is not "too much" time? Do you need to know how much time you are allocating? Do you feel free to discuss this with your partner?
- Are there any other emotional factors that I may have left out?

## 4. The State of the Relationship

Some people would not dream of being intimate when feeling estranged, unresolved, or disconnected. For others, physical intimacy is a way to reconnect and resolve conflict. How is it for you?

- What do you like to be happening between you and your partner before you are intimate? Some people enjoy intense intimacy after a fight. Others need to be quite connected to begin being physically close. How is it for you?
- What is the best way for you to feel connected before beginning to be intimate, if that is important to you?
- How is the decision to be intimate best made? Do you each feel free to say yes or no? Do you each feel free to agree on the time?
- How do you like to be approached? Do you respond best to spontaneity? Or do you like to plan ahead so you can orient yourself and prepare?
- Do you like a fairly patterned approach or do you like variety? People are very different about this too, and there is no "right" answer!
- Does your partner know how you most like to be touched? Do you like to be touched in certain ways and in a certain order?
- Do you like talking before or during intimate time? Or do you prefer to be nonverbal or silent?
- Did I forget anything? Of course! These questions are only a beginning to spark your own imagination, thoughts and feelings.

Answer the questions in writing privately. Then come together and discuss them with your partner.

## Chapter Eighteen

# WE'RE ON OUR WAY HOME: MORE ABOUT PRESENCE AND SOME PRACTICE

We continued to work on Anna staying present and in present time with her body experience. She discovered that when she was in her body (meaning tuned in and aware of her body sensations) and in the moment and when she knew what Larry was going to do so there was no element of surprise, she was free of pain. This was a great discovery: She could be physically comfortable and relatively calm. She could feel happily close to Larry. It was a big change. "I would like to *feel* something," she admitted, not wanting to sound ungrateful. She still did not yet feel anything remotely like erotic pleasure. We would return to this later.

As Larry began to access more and more of his history and his feelings, he increasingly knew and felt how deeply he longed to be wanted. He began to connect with the pain of that missing experience. In one of our sessions, Larry appeared uncharacteristically nervous. He said there was something he needed to talk about, certainly not that he wanted to. Both Anna and I were alerted that this would not be easy for him. Larry slowly eked out his words.

Sometimes after one of their wrenching bedtime episodes, when Anna was asleep, Larry told us, he would get up, go online, and look at porn. He would calm down by masturbating and then go back to bed. He felt angry and self-righteous about the episodes, but he also felt guilty and sad.

I asked Larry what sort of pictures he liked to look at. He said, "Nothing unusual or kinky. Mostly I like looking at pictures of women whose eyes and faces are lusty and burning with desire or who ravish their partners. That really turns me on."

"But there is something else about this that bothers me, that I need to come clean about," Larry added. "I used to feel the same way about prostitutes. I like not having to think about how the other person feels at all. I like having it be all about me, my orgasm, my pleasure, my time frame. I can fall asleep if I want to, I don't have to take care of anyone." He was horrified saying this out loud.

"Even if it is disturbing to you, Larry, everything you said does make a lot of sense." I explained to both of them, "Very often sexual fantasy and sexual tastes are tied in with early childhood experience or missing experience. It took great courage for you to tell us this."

The pictures enabled Larry to *imagine* feeling wanted after a lifetime of being unwanted and after a long stint of feeling unwanted and rejected by Anna. Since throughout his childhood, feeling it was pretty much always "all about her," it was deep in his nervous system to be sick to death of being so attentive and attuned to the other. He had told Anna he was "done" with doing that with her.

Although it took some effort, Anna could empathically see through Larry's eyes and to some extent understand what he had told us. She could not stomach the thought of pornography and she had not known that there had been a time in Larry's past when he visited prostitutes. But by now they had come far enough in their healing journey that she could feel compassion and even understanding. And she could see what it must mean that he was ready to reveal more about his 50 percent. Clearly he was acknowledging now that Anna did not own their problem. Just as Anna wanted to work deeply enough to access her own eroticism and passion with Larry, he was saying something similar about his own. They shared a powerful emotional moment. It is precisely moments like these where the most profound change occurs.

Both Larry and Anna felt deeply relieved, Anna because she was clearly no longer the "problem child," even about sex, in Larry's eyes, and Larry because he had divested himself of his "dirty secret" and Anna had not completely condemned and rejected him for it. He felt infinitely freer and more accepting of himself. "Funny thing," Anna said to Larry as the session came to a close. "Somehow your telling us this makes *me* feel more accepting of *myself* too!"

## SEE ME, FEEL ME, TOUCH ME, HEAL ME: WHAT SHALL WE CREATE?

Larry's divulging his sexual secret and expressing his shame put at least two other valuable entrees on our therapy table. One of them was the important issue of self-regulation. By now we know that both trauma and neglect dysregulate the nervous system, resetting it for hyperarousal or hypoarousal, anxiety or depression, or all of the above. The life of a traumatized person (be it shock trauma such as abuse or developmental trauma like neglect) is a chronic quest to self-regulate: to either calm down, feel alive, or both.

Children and adults are desperate and thus endlessly creative in the solutions they discover to make it bearable to exist in their skins. Drugs, alcohol, eating disorders, overworking, gambling, shopping, you get the idea. We knew that distance running was a way that Anna had found to self-regulate. For Larry as for many people, looking at pornography and masturbating was a stress reliever, a way to calm down. As is often the case, Larry was discovering that his method of calming down no longer sat well with him. It did not fit with the sexual relationship he was now creating with Anna, and it did not fit with the self-image that was emerging out of his deep personal work. This lead to the other important question that sprang from Larry's disclosure, "What sort of sexual relationship do we want to create?"

In her in-depth investigation of optimal sex mentioned earlier, sex therapist and researcher Peggy Kleinplatz sought to identify the specific elements that comprise great sex in self-described happy, sexually satisfied long-term monogamous couples. "Being present, focused, and embodied," was what Kleinplatz and her team found topping the list. "Being fully and completely present during sexual experiences was the component of great sex articulated first, foremost and most frequently by participants." So Anna and Larry agreed that working on that was indeed the way to go, not only for healing from trauma and neglect but also generically to have a top-quality erotic connection. So we continued the exploration of presence.

## A WORD ABOUT PRACTICE

Many of my clients have been daunted by or nervous about practice. That makes sense. There is a lot of water under that bridge, and it takes courage to begin the hands-on part of our journey. To ease the re-entry, I have a few suggestions. First, give time and thought to planning. I even tell couples who have a comfortable sexual relationship to give time and thought to planning. In these times, at least where I live, life is so hectic that if we don't carve out and protect time for important activities, they simply don't happen. Even happy couples with satisfying sex lives may find themselves "not getting around to it" because of the interference of so many other pursuits, especially if children are part of the mix. I recommend to everyone (including myself!) to allocate and protect time for intimacy. Spontaneity sounds good, but unfortunately it is not reliable enough.

How you approach practice sets the stage for how you will relate to your ongoing sexual relationship later. I recommend forging good habits like the following from the start:

- Create a harmonious and democratic way of negotiating decisions.
- Use what you learned about ideal conditions to orchestrate your practice.
- Make it both partners' responsibility to remember and honor the agreements around practice.
- Arrange your practice to be when you are rested, nourished, and free of other pre-occupations, with kids accounted for, phones turned off, and nothing on the stove.
- Agree in advance to a time frame and stick with it. Make sure it is sufficient (and not excessive) for both of you.
- Make sure your time allotment allows adequate (for both of you) time to get connected before you start and debrief when you finish.
- Some of the practices in this chapter are conversations that call for prior thought and preparation. Even with the best-laid plans (no pun intended!), they may be difficult. If you are in couples therapy, you may choose to have them with your therapist. Decide this together.
- *Don't* **ever** *do* **anything** *you don't want to do!* It is of course necessary to stretch beyond your comfort zone. But make sure you get to an honest "yes" before going forward with any activity. We *don't* want to create any new circuits or reinforce any old ones that embody any tinge of coercion!

Are you old enough to remember *Mr. Rogers' Neighborhood?* It was a children's TV show on PBS for many years. Mr. Rogers had a little song that I still remember from 45+ years ago. In his battered old cardigan and corny sneakers and with an earnest face, he used to sing, "You've got to learn your trade, everything takes practice! If you want to make the grade, you've got to practice practice!" I especially love this because the pun is that even practice takes practice!

---

### PRACTICE #2: GAZING

#### *Adapted from David Yarian, Tantra and Sex Therapy*

There are three variations of this practice. Try all three, not necessarily in the same session, although that is fine if you feel like it. Just make sure to allow plenty of time for each and for any discussion afterward. I suggest giving yourselves 20 to 30 minutes per session so you have time to settle, get connected, and debrief after each phase. Create the context using information gleaned from Practice 1 (The Ideal Time and Place).

#### Gazing Variation I: Remember Rabbi Hillel!

1. Sit facing your partner. Close your eyes and breathe. Feel your own body and your breath. Concentrate on being fully present with yourself. Feel your feet on the floor and the way

the floor and gravity support your feet and your weight. Feel the ground and your sense of being grounded. As you breathe, focus on staying connected with yourself and your breath.

2. Open your eyes to see your partner. Concentrate on staying connected with yourself and your breath. See if you can allocate as much energy to connecting with yourself as you do for connecting with your partner.

3. Place your hand on your heart as you look into your partner's eyes. Say quietly to yourself, "I am present with myself as I am present with you."

4. Close your eyes again. What do you notice about your connection with yourself as compared to the beginning of this gazing? What do you notice about your connection with your partner? Observe without judgment.

## Gazing, Variation II

1. Close your eyes. Feel your feet on the floor. Be fully present with yourself. Feel your breath.

2. Open your eyes to see your partner. When you do, see if you can stay connected to yourself as you send acceptance, love, and caring to your partner. Send that love and acceptance through your eyes into his/her eyes. Think about both seeing and being seen. Be present to yourself as you are present with your partner.

3. Close your eyes again. What do you notice?

## Gazing, Variation III

1. Close your eyes. Feel your feet on the floor beneath you. Be fully present with yourself. Feel your breath.

2. Open your eyes to see your partner. When you do, see if you can stay connected to yourself as you send acceptance, love, and caring to your partner. Send that love and acceptance through your eyes into his/her eyes. Think about both seeing and being seen. Be present to yourself as you are present with your partner.

3. Close your eyes again. What do you notice? Breathe and feel your breath.

4. Bring your awareness to your pelvic area. Focus on your sensations and energy in that area as you breathe. Feel your breath move the energy up through your body.

5. Open your eyes and see your partner again. Feel your breath move energy from your pelvis up through your body through your eyes and to your partner's eyes. Send energy with the love and acceptance into your partner's eyes. Breathe in and out, sending the love and energy back and forth eyes to eyes.

6. Close your eyes again. What do you notice?

These practices are worth doing again and again, as Mr. Rogers says; they are worth practicing. You may choose to come back in future sessions and repeat all three variations without clothes.

## PRACTICE #3: HEART FLOW

### *Adapted from David Yarian, Tantra and Sex Therapy*

This practice is another for working with presence and connecting simultaneously with your own and your partner's experience. This one includes touch.

1. Sit facing your partner, knees close or touching. Close your eyes and breathe. Feel your own body and your breath. Feel your feet on the floor and the way the floor and gravity support your seat in the chair, your feet, and your weight. As you breathe, focus on your heart area. See if you can feel the beating of your heart as you breathe. Feel your body calm as you breathe.
2. Slowly open your eyes and make eye contact with your partner. Gaze into your partner's eyes while still feeling your own breath and body. Feel the connection with yourself as you connect with your partner.
3. Place your left hand on your heart. While staying in eye contact with your partner, feel your own heart. Feel the connection with your partner as you feel your own heart.
4. Continue to breathe and feel your own body. Place your left hand on your partner's heart. Stay in eye contact with your partner. Place your right hand on your left hand. Feel your partner's heart beat under your hands.
5. Slowly synchronize your breath with your partner's breath. Breathe together. Feel the deep relaxation and the connection.
6. Concentrate on your breath and heart. Stay in eye contact. Imagine love flowing from your heart through your arm and down your hand into your partner's heart. Continue to feel your own heart as your partner's love flows into it. Stay in the flow for several minutes.

### Variations on Heart Flow

This practice also is worth doing again and again. Here are some variations of it to try later:

- Repeat the sequence lying down and facing one another.
- Repeat the sequence, placing first one open hand and then both of your hands, one atop the other, on your partner's breast.
- Repeat the sequence, placing first one open hand and then both of your hands, one atop the other, on your partner's groin.
- Try all the variations without clothing.

Chapter Nineteen

# STARTING OVER: PRACTICE AND MORE PRACTICE

When John Lennon and Yoko Ono got back together in the late 1970s after an explosive breakup, they produced their classic album *Double Fantasy*. I don't know Yoko's story, but John's early life was riddled with trauma. Sometimes when I am sitting with a couple who after a long and winding road have reached this stage, I'll hear John Lennon's voice joyfully echoing in my ears that when he sees his darling it is like falling in love all over again, that it is, as the song's title puts it, "(Just Like) Starting Over." And I privately smile as in my own little musical world I silently hum *wa wa wa wa* like the backup voices in the song's famous recording. It is a happy time when we reach this stage. The triggering is mostly behind us now. For the most part, trauma and neglect are finding their proper place in the past. Both partners are for the most part here and not there and are relating to each other instead of to ghosts.

Now there is more ease and more fun. There is more hope and more confidence. There is even pleasure now. Anna was delighted to discover that now in fact she did "feel" something, just as she had hoped to. First it had been the absence of pain. Then there was the sweetness of feeling emotionally close to Larry when they were physically close. And now there was a faint and growing whispering in her groin of pleasurable erotic sensation and even something akin to desire. Finally, there is more to life than therapy. Now there is practice. This chapter is primarily practice of various sorts.

## PRACTICE #4: GLORY DAYS: REMEMBERING THE POSITIVE

Perhaps there was a time in your relationship when the sex was going well or better, maybe at the beginning. This practice is a conversation. Begin by taking some time separately to ponder the questions.

(If there was not a time when your sexual relationship went well, no worries! Then have the conversation about your best times together of whatever sort. What are some of your happiest memories together? What was it like when you first got together?)

### Desire

Describe your level of desire. How did you experience it? How did you know that you wanted to be intimate? Did you have sensations in your body? Thoughts and fantasies of your partner and things you wanted to do to/with him or her? Or were you visited by memories of past times together?

### How Did Lovemaking Happen?

Who initiated? Did you have routines, times of day, rituals? Was it spontaneous or did you plan and premeditate it? What circumstances or preparation facilitated lovemaking?

### Meaning

What did the sexual interaction mean to you? Did it make you feel loved? Did it make you feel special to your partner? Did it signify commitment? Did it make you feel close and connected? Was it a way to keep yourself calm in general and manage your stress?

### What Did You Hope to Get Out of It?

Was sex a way to get closer? To relax? To get to sleep? Stress relief, anxiety relief? Relief from "horniness"? A way to get pregnant? Some combination of the above? What else?

### What Turned You on the Most?

The sight of your partner? Moments of intense emotional closeness/connection? Being touched in a certain way? Some other stimulus? What? Was it visual, auditory, a smell, or a taste? Was it a memory of a past interaction? Anticipation of something in particular? The passage of time?

### The Sexual Interaction Itself

Did you do different things together sexually then? Was there more mutual pleasuring? Did you share fantasy? Was there more looking? Gazing? Was there more kissing? Different positions? Play? Role play? Different venues? Out-of-town outings? Out of doors? A hot tub? By a fireplace? Did you linger afterward?

### Did You Allocate Time Together Differently Then?

Did you have date nights or days? Did you prioritize time alone together?

### What Do You Remember Most Fondly of This Sexual Time?

The sensory experience? The emotional experience? How you felt together afterward? Was there more nonsexual, affectionate touch outside of the lovemaking? How was that different? Did you talk to each other about your feelings? Was that different then?

When did you notice a change?

Notice what you feel right now as you recall all this. What is it like to "museum walk," to reminisce with your partner? What would you both like to resuscitate from those times? If you cannot remember a time like this with your partner, see if you can imagine what would make you feel most satisfied, happy, and fulfilled sexually. John and Yoko have some good ideas in the song "Starting Over," wa wa wa wa . . .

---

## WHERE DO WE GO FROM HERE?

A natural next step after remembering our best times is fashioning a vision of how we would like it to be together going forward. But careful! The stakes may seem so high as to feel like the pressure is on. If we think of getting the sexual relationship on track as a deal breaker, meaning if we don't resolve this we will have to break up, that can bring us to a freezing point. A freeze is a paralysis of terror, a trauma response resorted to when one cannot fight or flee an inescapable threat. If the prospect of breaking up looms as such a threat, it can be too frightening to even conceive of beginning. We want to calm the whole system down so we can move.

In addition to the challenge of concurrently being present to both self and partner, sex is a unique blend of arousal states. It requires that we be simultaneously relaxed *and* excited, calm *and* stimulated. Wow! It requires that we hold this tension of opposites in our bodies and emotions all at one time. Our practice requires a similar complex blend of states, that we be both dogged and intense in our approach to what is often challenging in all kinds of ways as well as patient and uncritically mindful and accepting. Practice also requires that we be should be searching and fearlessly self-reflective while also being attentive and empathic. What a feat! How do we do this? One possibility is to start with a reframe.

A reframe is finding a new way of thinking about something. Sex therapist Carol Ellison has redefined sex to be "Any erotic activity that is pleasurable, connecting, makes me feel good about myself, good about my partner and good about us." I like that redefinition or reframe because it shifts the emphasis off of performance and gives us a wide new berth for creativity and choice. To be sure, as we get older and our bodies change, creativity and flexibility around choices become not only wise but often also necessary!

At any age, however, I strive to combat a cultural view of sexuality that focuses on performance and results rather than presence, connection, and pleasure. A fixation on intercourse and orgasm is a narrow view. We aim for something much more expansive and, it is hoped, more relational. So as we start with a reframe definition of sex, what might yours be? Feel free to use this one, or tweak it so it fits you better. Think about it, maybe make some notes about it. You can keep them private if you like for now.

---

## PRACTICE #5: BACK IN THE HIGH LIFE AGAIN: MY SEXUAL VISION FOR ME AND FOR US

Practice #5 is another structured conversation that begins with individual reflection. What is your vision of yourself and yourselves, both as an individual partner and as an erotic partnership?

### Personal Vision: My Ideal Sexual Self

This one can be tricky, because if there is a tendency toward self-criticism or self-bashing, it might seep in here. And we don't want that! Rather, we are thinking about the question, "Who do I want to be sexually?" Of course we want to be realistic. I will never be JLo, and if I'm 5'5" now, I will only be 5'10" in my dreams. So we want to take it deeper than that.

Perhaps there was a time when you felt good about yourself sexually. What did you like about yourself? Did you feel ease and fluency about being sexual and confidence to flirt or initiate? Did you feel at home in your body? Perhaps you enjoyed dancing or some sort of sport where you felt your physical aliveness. Did you fantasize? Did you masturbate? Did you talk with your friends about sex? Read about it?

If there was a time when you felt comfort and/or pleasure around sexuality, see what you can remember about it. Reflect on it and make a few notes if you'd like. What parts of yourself from that time do you miss? What might you like to revive?

What kind of lover were you? Were you playful? Imaginative? Adventurous? Curious? Active or passive? Energetic? Were you more generous and interested then? Were you bolder? How much did you know about what you liked? How much did you communicate what you liked and what turned you on? Did you think ahead and plan for sexual interludes? Did you talk with your partner about sex?

If you don't have a pleasant memory or just don't remember much, *don't worry*! Many people don't. Then you can just use your grandest sexual organ, your imagination! Think about how you would most like to be sexually now. What is your greatest wish? Perhaps you want to feel freer or more relaxed. Perhaps you'd like to be more present or giving. Perhaps you'd like to be open enough to talk about sex or even talk during sex. Perhaps you'd like to play or even experiment with something a little on the kinky side. Maybe there are things you have always wanted to try. Perhaps you would just like to have the confidence to talk openly about any of this, without shame or embarrassment. Give some thought to this. Make a few notes.

### My Sexual Relationship Vision: My Ideal for Us

What are the qualities of a sexual relationship that you most wish for? (This is not meant to be a critique of your partner or yourself!)

### *Communication*

Do you want both of you to feel freer to talk about sexual matters—your feelings about things as well as details of what you do and don't like sexually? Is there much that goes unspoken between you about sex, which makes for confusion, tension, or a feeling of not being known or understood? Do you want to be able to talk more about what sex means to each of you? (Isabel Allende said, "For women, the best aphrodisiacs are words. The G spot is in the ears. He who looks for it below there is wasting his time." Is that true for you?)

### *Intimacy*

Do you wish for the whole endeavor to be more intimate? What does that mean? More talking? More nonerotic, affectionate touch? Does sex feel divorced from emotional closeness or devoid of emotion? Does it feel mechanical to you? Does it seem to you that there is little connection between the sexual activity and the rest of your relationship life? Does sex feel mutual to you? Does it feel to you as if sex honors you both? What do we mean by "honoring"?

### *Romance*

Do you wish for more fuss, more fanfare, more surprises, more gifts, more seduction? Are there trappings that would make sex feel more special to you or would make you feel more special? Do you like special garments, environments, accoutrements? Outings or rituals around sex?

### *Priority*

Does sex hold an important place in your life together? Is it too important? Is it important enough? Do you both make time for it and look forward to it? Do you each bring your best self to the encounter most of the time?

### Orgasm

Do you have orgasms? How important are orgasms to you? To your partner? Do you feel responsible for your partner's orgasm? Do you feel responsible for your own? Do you feel pressure from your partner to have an orgasm? Would your partner feel let down if you didn't? Would you? Do you like to be involved in your partner's orgasm? Do you prefer to have your partner involved in yours? Do you like flexibility around this? How do you feel about masturbation (both together and separately)? Is masturbation something you can talk about? Do you want that to be part of your sexual relationship "menu?" What about vibrators or other toys or equipment?

### Foreplay

What is your idea of foreplay? Does it ideally begin outside the bedroom for you? Hours beforehand? Days?

### Variety

Play, role play, kink, nontraditional arrangements: would you want an expanded menu? Do you prefer the tried and true, and does repetition feel cozy to you? Do you feel the relationship is sufficiently open and nonjudgmental to talk about things like this?

### What Else?

Of course this list is not exhaustive! It is meant to stimulate your own imagination. Give your vision some thought. Maybe make some notes. Then arrange a time for conversation. This practice may involve many conversations! I suggest blocking out 45 to 60 minutes at a time, but probably not more. It may be stressful or tiring, and you don't want to overwhelm yourself or your partner.

If you are in couples therapy or sex therapy, you may choose to include your therapist in the conversation. Don't rush these musings, and remember they most likely will be a work in progress throughout your life, just like most other things!

---

## PRACTICE #6: I WANNA COME OVER! INITIATING, RESPONDING, AND "SEDUCTION RITUALS"

Many partners in couples I see have shame, pain, or resentment surrounding initiating sex. Many may feel anxiety, fear, and pressure around responding to the initiative. They may have unfortunate nagging residual patterns or apprehension about how sex will begin. We want to begin afresh.

People vary widely about how they like to be invited into sexual interaction. Some like to be seduced. Others like to feel it is mutual right from the start. Some like on-a-dime spontaneity. Others like plenty of time to orient and prepare psychologically and physically. Some like rough-and-tumble play around sex; others prefer gentle sweetness and romance or more somber connecting. Some must feel connected and close before getting started with sexual intimacy or they might feel like an object. For others, sexual intimacy is *the* way to get close and connected. There are countless possibilities, as many as there are people! An interlude can be royally spoiled or an opportunity for intimacy instantly missed if we initiate or ask in a way that rubs our partner the wrong way! It is well worth learning what works and does not work for you and your partner so you have a better shot at hitting the mark and are less likely to get your feelings hurt!

*Of course, every couple must be assured that both partners have the freedom to invite and equal liberty to accept or decline sex for any reason.* The only true and authentic "yes" assumes the equal freedom of a true and authentic "no." We are all vulnerable in different ways. Some "nos" feel gracious, empathic, and sensitive, where others feel stinging, rejecting, or nasty. Again, we are all different about this! Learning how to gracefully and kindly initiate, accept, or decline makes the relationship safer for both partners. It becomes less risky to ask if the other's response is caring. And if my "no" is kind, your "no" about this or other things is likely to be kinder, too.

Many couples who struggle around this issue have historically had one partner who has typically been the pursuer and the other the distancer around sex. In the initiating and responding practice, both partners will try on both roles. Each partner will initiate, accept, and decline.

This is a role-play activity. You might say, "Ughhh . . . role playing!" I encourage you to give it a try! I won't ask you to have fun with it, but hey, there's a chance . . .

The activity has four parts. I suggest you break it into two sessions.

## Session I: Initiating

## Allow about 15 minutes for each segment of Session 1.

### Segment 1: Initiating

**Partner A** demonstrates "My ideal vision of how you would invite me to make love with you." (In showing you how I'd like you to do it, in effect I am role playing or "being" you! Just for a little while!)

You may not have thought this through before, so you may not have a good idea of what would be your most positive invitation style. Take your time. Let your imagination go. Include facial expression, body language, touch (or not), tone of voice, cadence, emotional tone, facial expression, imaginary props.

**Partner B**, the Invitee: Just listens with nondefensiveness. As recipient of your partner's desired invitation style, you also are in a position to step into your partner's world, see and listen through your partner's eyes and ears. You are also in effect "being your partner," just for a little while!

Prepare yourself. Perhaps what you will hear will be something you think you have tried before. Maybe you think you have tried it a million times! See what you notice inside as you listen, what emotions and possible triggers. What sparks emotion or anxiety? Where do you feel them in your body? Do your best to contain them and see what you can feel and learn about yourself and about your partner.

Take time to talk before continuing.

### Segment 2: Initiating

Switch roles. Partner B demonstrates as Partner A did above "My ideal vision of how you would invite me to make love with you." Partner A becomes the invitee. Instructions to both partners will be as above.

### What to Strive for in All Four Segments

Be kind!
Give your partner more than words to work with!
Include gesture, facial expression, physical movements, and touch.
Be as detailed and specific as you can!
Take it slow!

### What to Avoid in All Four Segments

Make your best effort to avoid telling your partner (again!) all the ways he or she has blown it in the past. If there are specific behaviors that you fear may trigger you, express this gently, lovingly, and carefully! Even in role play, this is vulnerable material!

After completing Segments 1 and 2, rest! Talk about how you felt in each role and what you learned about yourself and about your partner. Discuss when you might have some real-life practice of what you learned. Remember, even if you replicate perfectly what you have been shown, it is not a guarantee that you will always get a "yes"!

End the session with expressions of appreciation.

### Session II: Responding

### Allow 20 minutes for each segment.

(This session is harder and has more components.)

### Segment 3: Responding

Partner A demonstrates both an ideal acceptance and an optimal declining of the invitation. Again, Partner A is showing Partner B "This is how I would like you to respond to my overture to you." So again, in this segment Partner A is "being" Partner B. What emotions do you notice, and what do you notice in your body when you say "yes?" When you say "no?"

Partner B, notice what happens inside when you hear the "yes," when you hear the "no." Of course, remember what you are being shown is how your partner would like you to accept or decline. Can you imagine responding as your partner is asking you to? What emotions do you feel when you think about that? What do you feel in your body?

Take time to talk before continuing.

### Segment 4: Responding

Reverse roles and do the same.

After completing segments 3 and 4, rest!

Talk about how you felt in each role and what you learned about yourself and about your partner.

End your sessions with expressions of appreciation.

Do you feel empowered now that you know what might work? Hopeful?

Discuss when you might have some real-life practice of what you learned.

### Suggestions

I recommend both partners getting into the following habit: if you decline an actual (as opposed to role-played) overture, offer *some* alternative (which of course your partner is under *no* obligation to accept). For example, "I'm not up for lovemaking right now. Is there some way I could pleasure you that you would enjoy instead?" Or "How about we cuddle and fall asleep together? Would that be another way we could be close?" I would avoid an alternative time such as "How about tomorrow night?" because there may be a history of "mañana" never materializing or struggles with procrastination that make such postponements difficult to trust. Is there something you could do now?

When you practice what you have learned about initiating and responding:

### Thoughts for the Responder

- Notice how you feel hearing your partner initiate in the way you said you would prefer.
- What emotions do you notice? What do you notice in your body?
- Do you feel excited and appreciative about your partner hearing your requests?
- Do you find yourself listening for a "mistake" or expecting your partner to forget what is important to you?
- Do you feel touched about being seen and heard in a way that makes you want to please your partner?
- Do you feel obligated, because your partner is accommodating you, to accept the invitation?

These are just some possibilities. What else?

### Thoughts for the Initiator

- Notice how you feel initiating, to the best of your ability, using what you think you learned from your partner in the prior session.
- Do you feel anxious about getting it exactly right?

- Do you fear that if you don't initiate "perfectly" you'll lose your "one chance?"
- Does it seem to you that you only have one chance?
- What other emotions might you have about initiating your partner's way?
- Do you feel angry or controlled?
- Does it "cramp your style?" Or make you not want to bother?
- Do you feel happy and empowered knowing what your partner might like?
- Again, even if you do exactly what your partner requests, there is no guarantee of a "yes" response every time.

---

## PRACTICE #7: THE MAGICAL MYSTERY TOUR: A GUIDED BODY TOUR

*Adapted from a practice I learned from sex therapist*
*Linda Alperstein*

What do you know about how you'd like to be touched that you would like to tell your partner? Perhaps you know a lot about what you like; perhaps you don't know that much. This is an activity to help you safely explore *talking* to your partner about how you might like to be touched and learn the same about him or her.

A suggested length for each session is about 10 to 15 minutes. But this may seem too long or too short to you and your partner. Make a joint decision before you begin and have both of your turns be the same length. The listener will be the timekeeper.

Remember: *Touch varies from occasion to occasion! Nothing is fixed.* One person can touch you in a particular place on your body and you feel tickled. You might be touched in that same place by a different person or on a different day and feel tortured, or you might feel nothing at all. Responses may vary widely and change at different times, with different moods or people, and under different circumstances. Even what you discover from this exploration can shift and change!

### Session 1

The first session is verbal only and you are in clothes. One partner at a time will be the speaker. The tour will be only above the waist.

Choose a quiet, comfortable, pleasant place to be together. Make sure you have plenty of privacy and plenty of undisturbed time. Make sure phones are turned off, the kids are all right, and that your attention is fully available.

*Remember!* If at any point either listener or speaker is upset, *stop*! Relax, breathe, let yourselves settle. Either take a break or stop completely. In order to ensure safety for both of you, it is essential that either partner be free to ask to stop for *any* reason.

#### Instructions to Speaker

Start with the top of your head.

Tell your partner how you like to be touched on your head. Do you like to be rubbed, patted, massaged, scratched, have your hair stroked, kissed? Give as much detail as possible about how you like to be touched on the top of your head, demonstrating on yourself if you wish.

Next, your face:

How do you like to be touched on your face? Do you like to be gently stroked, lightly, or a stronger touch? Kissed? Your eyes and eyebrows? Your lips in particular? What about your ears? (For some the ears are very sensitive; for others they are ticklish. And for some they are just neutral! We are all different.) Under your chin? Go slowly if you haven't thought about this.

Then to your neck:

Do you like to be kissed on the neck? Do you like to be stroked on the back of the neck? The side of the neck? Do you like deep stroking or feathery light? With any part of your body, imagine that part has a voice. Would it say, "Touch me hard" or "Touch me soft" with the fingers or with the whole hand? Use as much description as possible.

Then the shoulders, in as much detail as possible, and continue along down.

Arms. Don't forget the inside of the elbows, which can be very sensitive for some people!

Chest and breasts:

Nipples can be very erotic for some people, both male and female. Others find touch to the nipples to be annoying. What parts of the chest and breasts are most sensitive in a positive way? Or does touch there feel too ticklish or painful? Perhaps you like massage of the chest and/or breast.

Back:

Either turn or point to areas of your back. Are there any ticklish spots on your back? *Remember, often what is ticklish is a most sensitive area depending on the mood.*

Include your rib cage, both the front and the sides.

Stop at the waist.

### Instructions to Listener

Pay close attention. You can ask questions. Notice if and when you start to get anxious. Where in your body do you experience that?

Don't disagree. Do your best to contain your own reaction.

Even if something contradicts what your partner has told you before, just listen.

At the end of the session, Speaker, thank your partner for listening.

Listener, thank your partner for sharing this intimate information with you.

Take a 5- to 30-minute break together for a cup of tea or a stretch, and relax. Don't switch too fast. We don't want this to feel like work! And you need time to absorb the experience.

After your break, switch roles.

### After Session 1

Make mental or written notes that you can refer to and use to remind yourself of what you are learning. If you are in couples therapy or sex therapy, you may want to bring them to your session to discuss. Make a point of noticing specifically when you noticed yourself becoming anxious and how you experienced that anxiety in your body.

You will probably want to repeat Session 1 a time or two before proceeding to Session 2. You may even find it interesting, enjoyable, and fun!

## Guided Body Tour

### *Session 2*

The purpose of the Body Tour is twofold (at least!). The first is obvious: learning about each of your preferences for touch. The second is about working with feelings and arousal. By now you are familiar with emotional feelings and somewhat practiced at learning to identify and tolerate those. So what do we mean by *arousal*?

By *arousal* we mean more than the sexual sensations of getting turned on or sexual arousal. We also mean arousal in the more general sense, which is all the ways the body starts to rev up, be it with excitement, anxiety, anger, fear, pressure, or anything else. *The idea is to begin to learn about your own and your partner's different kinds of arousal.*

In the case of your own arousal, the challenge is to notice and begin to manage it. By learning to notice where and how it starts and getting and developing tolerance for how it feels, you will gain control, feel safer, and learn to keep yourself calm and comfortable. That's the idea!

In the case of your partner's arousal, of course, you will be learning more about your partner and what makes for a safe, pleasurable, and hopefully connecting experience for both of you. This, of course, requires a high level of awareness. So as you approach this activity, make sure that you are in an undistracted frame of mind. Again, make sure it is a good time. Plan together to optimize your success!

*In general, being able to concentrate and being able to focus on feeling body sensation are key ingredients in any kind of positive sensual or sexual experience.*

Before Beginning Session 2

This session is a continuation of the waist-up tour. This time, however, you will both be naked from the waist up. Where Session 1 was an activity that was primarily verbal, this session may include touch. You will work out together how you would like to demonstrate the touch. You will agree together if you would like to demonstrate the touch on your own bodies or guide the listener's hand on your body when you are the speaker. Take your time working that out together. You may choose to first do a complete tour demonstrating on yourself and the next time guiding your partner's hand. Take your time working it out and planning. *Remember, surprises can be startling and can definitely break a mood!* Keep both of yourselves safe by making clear agreements at the outset.

Before beginning the tour, notice what it is like to be naked together from the waist up. Perhaps you are used to seeing each other naked in daylight. Perhaps not. Notice your own anxiety or excitement about this. Do you feel more about seeing your partner or about being seen?

How do you experience these feelings in your body? Where in your body do you notice them?

Take your time with this. Breathe. Make eye contact. See how that feels. *Don't rush into starting the activity!*

Remember these feelings and jot them down at the end of the tour session. You may choose to talk about them with your partner later. If you are in therapy, that would also be a good place to discuss them.

Again, choose a quiet, comfortable, pleasant place to be together. Make sure you have plenty of privacy and plenty of undisturbed time. Make sure phones are turned off and that your attention is fully available.

*Again, remember!* If at any point either listener or speaker is upset, *stop!* Relax, breathe, let yourselves settle. Either take a break or stop completely. In order to ensure safety for both of you, it is essential that either partner be free to ask to stop for *any* reason. Defer the conversation until our next therapy session.

Decide together how long the sessions will be. Allow more time for Session 2 than Session 1, because you may need to go more slowly and allow more time for your feelings.

The listener will be the timekeeper.

Instructions to Speaker

You as speaker may choose to show your partner what you like by touching your own body. Or you may prefer to take your partner's hand or hands and demonstrate the touch on your own body by guiding your partner's hand(s). Decide this together *before you begin*.

If you do choose to guide your partner's hands on your body, be gentle and patient. Most likely both of you are feeling sensitive, vulnerable, and perhaps anxious. Be aware of your own feelings. Try and spot exactly when they start up and where in your body you feel them. If your partner is not quite "getting it," make the adjustments in an uncritical way. Eye contact and smiles will help both of you!

Start with the top of your head.

Show your partner how you like to be touched on your head. Do you like to be rubbed, patted, massaged, scratched, have your hair stroked, kissed? Give as much detail as possible about how you like to be touched on the top of your head, demonstrating on yourself or guiding your partner's hand(s).

Notice what feels different being undressed from the waist up, even though the focus is now still on an area that is not normally covered. Anything different about how you like your head touched when you are naked from the waist up? Any difference in how the touch feels now?

Next, your face:

How do you like to be touched on your face? Do you like to be gently stroked, lightly or a stronger touch? Kissed? Your eyes and eyebrows? Your lips in particular? What about your ears? (For some the ears are very sensitive for others they are ticklish. And for some they are just neutral! We are all different.) Under your chin? Go slowly.

Again, notice what feels different being undressed from the waist up, even though the focus is still on an area that is not normally covered. Anything different about how you like your face touched when you are naked from the waist up? Any difference in how the touch feels now?

Then to your neck:

Do you like to be kissed on the neck? Do you like to be stroked on the back of the neck? The side of the neck? Do you like deep stroking or feathery light? With any part of your body, imagine that part has a voice. Would it say, "Touch me hard" or "Touch me soft" with the fingers or with the whole hand? Demonstrate.

Again, notice what is different now from when you were dressed. Track your emotions and sensations. Take your time!

Then the shoulders, in as much detail as possible, and continue along down.

Arms. Don't forget the inside of the elbows, which can be very sensitive for some people!

Chest and breasts:

Nipples can be very erotic for some people, both male and female. Others find touch to the nipples to be annoying. What parts of the chest and breasts are most sensitive in a positive way? Or does touch there feel too ticklish or painful? Perhaps you like massage of the chest and/or breast.

Because breasts can be very sexy for many men and women, go especially slowly with this and notice as much as you can. You may both be having a lot of feelings!

Back:

Either turn or point to areas of your back. Are there any ticklish spots on your back? Remember, often what is ticklish is most sensitive, depending on the mood.

Rib cage, front and sides:

Stop at the waist.

Instructions to Listener

Pay close attention. You can ask questions. Notice when you start to get anxious. Where in your body do you experience that?

Don't disagree. Do your best to contain your own reaction.

Even if something contradicts what your partner has told you before, just listen.

*Take special care if your partner is guiding your hand(s) on his or her body* to really follow the guidance. It is an act of faith to share this information with you, so honor that!

At the end of the session, Speaker, thank your partner for following/listening.

Listener, thank your partner for guiding/sharing this intimate information with you.

Take a 5- to 30-minute break together for a cup of tea or a stretch, and relax. Don't switch too fast.

After your break, switch roles.

### After Session 2

Put on a robe or something comfortable and jot down what you noticed from the session. What areas of your body awakened the most feelings, sensations, and arousal of all kinds in you? What areas of your partner's body? What part of the activity was the most interesting and informative? What did you learn? What was the most pleasant? How so? What was the most difficult or unpleasant? What made it unpleasant, and what did it feel like, emotionally and in your body?

Make a special point of noticing specifically when you started becoming most anxious and how you experienced that anxiety in your body.

### Continue the Tour

Once you've done structured Sessions 1 and 2 a number of times, you have the concept of the Body Tour. Often couples repeat them many times before going further and come to enjoy repeating and practicing what they now know. When you are ready, together you can design the subsequent sessions and how you will introduce or reintroduce each other to more and more intimate parts of yourselves and your bodies.

When you arrive at erogenous zones, let each other know what words you like to use for your body parts. Some people are most comfortable with formal terms like *penis* and *vagina*. Others like coarser terms like *cock* and *pussy*. Some have their own little names or learned words in their childhoods for body parts. (When I was growing up, the word my mother used for buttocks was *popo*, with the accent on the second syllable.) Find the language that works for both of you just as you find the pace that works for both of you.

I suggest you have at least one practice a week. Remember that the way you make and keep to a regular rhythm of practice creates a template for making time for lovemaking. These are good habits to develop!

---

## PRACTICE #8: DANCING IN THE DARK: SENSATE FOCUS

In the 1950s with the advent of sex therapy, Masters and Johnson developed the practice of what they called sensate focus. The objective was to take the emphasis off of intercourse and orgasm and just relax into the enjoyment of sensual erotic touch. This is our next practice.

Using what you learned about each other's likes and preferences, block out an agreed-upon length of time to be together and touch each other. The idea is to explore, feel close, feel pleasure, have fun, feel good about yourself, good about your partner, and good about the relationship. Make sure you are both clear that intercourse and orgasm are not on the menu. One couple I worked with affectionately referred to this as "hangout time." I like that term because it suggests an airy freedom from pressure and expectation. Do things you enjoy before and after, talking, dancing, taking a shower, eating, playing games, whatever is relaxing and connecting to you both.

I suggest repeating this practice at least weekly until you find yourselves feeling really comfortable. Keep your conversations going about how you are feeling things are progressing. Be patient with each other and any differences in timing and ease. Follow each session with expressions of appreciation.

## I'LL BE YOUR BABY TONIGHT: MAKING LOVE AGAIN

If you haven't made love in a while, you will probably know when you are both ready. Keep the communication open and clear: keep talking about how things are going. I suggest that you decide together and plan. By now you have a wealth of information about what is ideal in terms of time and place and in terms of touch. You really have everything you need now. Mix it up with both of your preferences. Make sure you are relaxed, connected and rested and have plenty of time.

Make of it a homecoming! Our main objective is that you both feel comfortable, safe, and connected to yourselves and each other. Have fun! Wa wa wa wa.

Chapter Twenty

# WHAT A LONG, STRANGE TRIP IT'S BEEN: INTEGRATION, "RE-MEMBERING," AND RENEWAL

The Talmud teaches "the long way is the short way, and the short way is the long way." This journey we have been mapping is circuitous, rocky, and most likely a long one. Of course, when we think in terms of attachment styles and brain circuits that hearken back to the first breaths of life, it stands to reason that the changes take longer than we would like. Still, it irks me mightily that children of neglect and trauma who suffer pain and indignities through their early years must then expend buckets of sweat and tears, and often thousands of dollars, just to reach the point of being able to live calmly and (hopefully) joyfully in their skins. Satisfying love and sexual freedom are your birthrights as a human being. These deep convictions inspire me to seek out the swiftest and most effective routes to healing, cutting only corners that we safely can. That is what I most wish for you. This departing chapter is like one last sweep of the hotel room before heading out. Have I missed anything?

The intimate partnership takes us to our depths like nothing else, that is, no one can trigger you right to the quick of your trauma like your partner can! On the other hand, the power of that catalyst coupled with the intensity of the drive to attach and love combine into an unbeatable elixir. I view healing in the relationship as absolutely the most direct way. And best of all, at the end of the day, you get to take the healing relationship home with you! It is probably also the single best thing you can do for your own children, born or as of yet unborn.

But I won't lie to you, it will be the toughest thing you ever do, even if it is the most rewarding.

Most often, concurrent individual therapy alongside this work is an added boon. For many, it is a necessary adjunct. We now know that trauma and neglect involve profound dysregulations of the nervous system and that as a result of these experiences, left-brain functions such as reasoned, analytical thinking and verbalization may log off during the actual trauma itself and subsequent activations of it. For these reasons, brilliant, dogged, and creative clinicians and researchers in the subfield of trauma therapy have evolved therapeutic methods that involve more than traditional talk therapy. I do recommend venturing outside the familiar box, as you probably learned to do long ago, and looking into them. I list some approaches I like in the appendix.

## DON'T YOU FORGET ABOUT ME!: "RE-MEMBERING"

In his valuable discussion of sexual healing, Peter Levine recounts the Greek myth of Isis, whose beloved husband Osiris has been murdered by his enemies and torn limb from limb. The ravaged parts of his body are strewn throughout the town. Isis is of course devastated and bereft. In an attempt to begin to reconstitute herself and emerge from her immense grief and loss, she goes about the town and gathers back the scattered pieces of him. Levine calls this "re-membering," or reassembling of the dismembered pieces, the essence of healing.

The journey of overcoming trauma and abuse, healing relationship, and restoring sexuality is all about this re-membering. This is not so much in terms of recalling painful memory as mending fragmentation and integrating the various parts and aspects. As Carol, a client of mine long ago, once said, "Recovery is like putting a clock back together." Trauma is shattering. Healing is bringing all the springs and cogs into a new working harmony. Often, like Isis, we must scavenge widely to recover all the essential parts.

Celeste, a bright, lively, and charismatic young artist I once worked with, had an irascible flying phobia. Although adventurous in countless ways, she had not set foot on an airplane in virtually all of her adult life. As a small child, her divorced, wealthy parents lived in different, distant cities. Weekdays she lived in Baltimore with her emotionally abusive, alcoholic mother. For the weekends she was sent off to Hartford to be with her sadistic, sexually abusive father. From the age of 4 years old, airplanes delivered her from one horror to the other. Needless to say, as soon as she was old enough to have a choice, she steered clear of both parents and airplanes, too.

Celeste worked hard in therapy to overcome her trauma and created much peace and happiness for herself. She became a deeply spiritual person, as reflected in her art. She created a community of close friends to soften the absence of a loving family. She completed an exclusive art school and contemplated graduate school. We reached a point where the last frontier that remained to be conquered was her fear of flying. Celeste wanted to see the world, even had the means, but she was petrified to even contemplate the airport.

As we approached her obstacle to flying, it slowly became clear that some part of Celeste, a hurt little girl part, feared that if she resolved this last symptom and actually lived the life of contentment she had so striven to create, somehow it would be as if nothing had happened to her. The evidence would evaporate. Her parents would be free and clear of any responsibility. Celeste realized she was keeping the flying phobia almost as a monument to her suffering, a tribute to the hurt child, or as *proof* that she had been wronged. This is true for many other traumatized people. Working with Vietnam veterans, I saw something similar. If they resolved their horrific nightmares, they felt as if they were abandoning or betraying their buddies who had been killed in the war.

For some couples, the sexual impasse may serve as just such a monument. Because sexuality is so complex and challenging, it often by default remains as the last frontier and in this same way digs its heels in. It is as if having a joyful life denies history. Many Holocaust survivors have lived out their whole lives in depression for this reason.

Once Celeste recognized this, we set about building a monument *outside of her* to memorialize her past. Using her art, she created a symbol, a poignant sculpture of the hurt little girl, shuttled back and forth between two hells, and honored that. The sculpture held her story for her, so she did not have to keep living it. We were then able to work through her flying phobia. Subsequently, she proceeded to jet about the world and even got into a long-distance relationship that involved frequent flights across the country. Ultimately she no longer needed to memorialize the hurt child anymore. Eclipsed by her full life, her trauma ceased to be the defining aspect of her identity and receded into quiet memory.

It is worth asking: "Might some part of me be holding on to the sexual impasse as a monument?" It might be a monument to terrible events from childhood and/or to terrible times in this relationship. Of course, Celeste was *not* retaining the symptom consciously or intentionally. By bringing it to awareness, she became able to work with it. As ever, it is essential to approach this question without blame or self-blame! Then, as with Celeste, the way can be cleared for freedom.

## I'M LOSING YOU: A NEW TWIST ON SEPARATION ANXIETY

Another variation of the snag around completion can be this one: Sometimes just at the verge of making a huge surge of progress, couples find themselves in a puzzling regression that may look like a backslide. Looking at each other, they wonder, "How are we here again?" It may be that they are making a confusing foray into a variation on separation anxiety.

Those of you who are parents are familiar with the phenomenon of freeze or even panic that might come over a child when he or she is first left with another caregiver. Attachment research has taught us that even when relationships are fraught with ambivalence, the bonds are unconscious, sticky, and deep. Disconnection from primary attachment figures can be surprisingly frightening. Something similar can happen when adults are truly changing. There is a way that they are breaking all the family rules. By having a safe, open, and deeply intimate partnership, even one that includes loving sexual relating, on some level one partner or both might feel as if they are leaving their families behind. And they are! Much as this may be what they most want to do, it may on some level also be terrifying. They might not even know that they are afraid or what is going on, just that they are anxious, irritable, or volatile. One partner might view the other as sabotaging.

Try to understand this as unintentional, unconscious, and natural. And work with the frightened parts of your partner and yourself as if you were working with that fearful child venturing off to preschool. What that child needs is gentle and reassuring support through a normal developmental passage. With reassurance, understanding, and time, children happily make the transition into growth, maturity, and a wonderful new stage. Validating the fear and lending strength, patience, and wisdom will steady the step of the little one, the adult, or the couple. Then the change can take root.

## DISMANTLING THE FORTRESS: GETTING TO INTERDEPENDENCE

Carl and Diana had never really had sex in their 11-year partnership. Early in their relationship when they attempted to be intimate, Diana's full-blown panic stopped the action, which had never resumed. Although Carl had been single much of his adult life, he'd had some prior relationships. Since he had never had any sexual difficulty in any of those, he was "comfortable" in his belief that the sexual problem resided with Diana. He had turned off to her sexually, not only because her terror response had rattled and made him feel guilty but also because after that, he could not quite see her as a sexual being anymore.

Diana was striking in an exotic, somewhat mysterious way. As she worked and emerged from her trauma and became calmer and happier, she seemed to grow more and more beautiful. Yet somehow Carl still harbored a gnawing worry about committing to a future with Diana. They had been faced with all sorts of major challenges beyond their childhoods, including professional, medical, and economic trials. They had endured and prevailed, yet still Carl was hesitant and doubtful as to whether a passionate and satisfying sex life was possible for them. He hovered on the fence.

Carl asked to do have a few sessions alone with me. There were some things he wanted to explore and understand better individually before expressing them to Diana. In those sessions Carl heroically plumbed his depths to understand his ambivalence. What we uncovered was another sort of terror. Quintessential child of neglect, Carl had successfully constructed a fortresslike existence where he did not need anyone for anything. Although he was pretty isolated and sometimes distressed about his anxiety in relationships, solitude, autonomy, and self-reliance were his comfort zone. Diana's trauma provided a convenient explanation for the distance and sexual disconnection between them. Carl took care of his sexual needs alone and maintained a level of separateness that could be mistaken for accommodating to Diana's trauma. It was a grand and blinding collusion until Diana's healing began to crack the façade. Carl's 50 percent became undeniable, even to them.

In order to open to his desire for Diana, Carl would have to disarm his primary survival strategy. He would have to risk opening to his need for another person, possibly risking the kind of devastation that he had experienced in childhood and spent his entire subsequent life mobilized to prevent. Did he have the courage to allow himself to wake up to real love and interdependence? That was the big question that, once faced with it, squarely impelled the needed change. Not easily, mind you!

Unlike his entire life up until now, there was an alternative to the only two possibilities he had ever known: flight or endurance. Carl did not have to work it out alone. With an 11-year investment already in, and with Diana's compassionate support, he opted to take his chances. I told Carl something I have seen over and over again, both in my own life and in the lives of individuals and couples I see every day. You just can't imagine what you can't imagine! Small steps, a day at a time, are the way there.

Sex therapist Barry McCarthy has wisely said that when there is a sexual problem, sex represents about 80 percent of the relationship's appraised health or unhealth. When sex is good, it represents about 10 percent! I have often seen that once the sexual relationship comes back online and all is relatively well, the partner who was endlessly unhappy and chronically complaining about the lack of sex does not in fact desire it all that often and may even turn out to be the lower-desire partner. Go figure . . .

## I WON'T BACK DOWN: STAYING THE COURSE

Although the roadmap may fit tidily and concisely into these pages, in actuality our journey can be anything but tidy and concise. It can in fact involve periods of arduous and intense slogging that may feel like stasis or even going backward, particularly at the earlier stages of work where the cycles of escalation are still frequent and fierce. I have rarely seen people who are truly stuck, but sometimes you may *feel* as if you are. When all of us are making the earnest effort, however, although things may appear to slow down, they rarely become static. Often they hover at a sticky place when a breakthrough is in the offing.

As a lifelong endurance athlete, I learned early that it is essential to find a pace that I could maintain for the long haul. Drink plenty of water and Gatorade, stay adequately nourished, get enough rest, wear a helmet, you get the idea. Think of this as a distance event, your own Tour de France. Some essential inputs besides the obvious good nutrition, sleep, and hydration are required: humor, support, the preferred nutrients of *your* soul, be they rock and roll, exercise, meditation, nature, or dogs . . . And I recommend getting the best help you can. The long way is in fact the short way. Don't skimp on self-care!

## DON'T STOP BELIEVING: COMING HOME TO PASSION

Relationship research produced the concept of positive sentiment override. When each partner contributes generously to the positive savings account in their positive-to-negative ratio, the couple is more resilient. The extra reserve of positive provides a buffer against what could otherwise rupture them. Little irritants have less destabilizing impact and a potentially triggering episode might fizzle rather than explode. Cycles of escalation are "metabolically expensive," wear both partners out (not to mention their adrenal glands!), and can erode both hope and good will.

Whatever positive inputs you can inject into the relationship environment have an amazing impact on moving things along. I have seen couples so deeply in the red for appreciation and kindness from each other that the simple act of focusing on expressing the positive powerfully begins to turn the boat around. Generosity begets generosity, and the delightful momentum of a positive escalation gathers steam and grows. Don't wait for your partner to start a positive cycle. The one who benefits most is you!

I take as given that the endeavor of healing trauma and neglect and healing your relationship will be the centerpiece of your life for a time. That is normal, and it won't be so forever. Ultimately you will emerge from a life of working on your relationship to a life of living it.

In closing we return to Rabbi Hillel, who standing on one foot proclaimed, "If I am not for myself, who will be for me? If I am only for myself, what good am I? If not now, when? That is the whole Torah; all the rest is commentary. Now go and study!" Here is the one-footed advice I will give: Nourish a partnership with someone who is really willing to work on the relationship with you, through the lifespan, to inhabit his or her own yard and really clean up that side of the street. If both of you are willing to do that, the sky is the limit. All the rest is commentary! Now, go and practice!

# APPENDIX

## RESOURCES FOR HEALING
### Trauma and Neglect

Cominghometopassion.com
Website with a collection of articles on many subjects relevant to this book and a link to contact the author.

Eegspectrum.com
Site providing information about neurofeedback, an approach to self-regulation therapy that is highly effective with trauma and neglect.

Emdria.org
Site of the EMDR International Association. Eye movement desensitization and reprocessing (EMDR) is a treatment approach effective with trauma.

Sensorimotorpsychotherapy.org
Site of Pat Ogden's sensorimotor psychotherapy, a powerful treatment methodology for treating trauma.

Traumacenter.org
The state-of-the-art Boston research and treatment program run by Dr. Bessel van der Kolk.

Traumahealing.com
Site of Peter Levine's somatic experiencing, a powerful treatment methodology for healing trauma.

Trauma-pages.com
A massive online library of information about trauma and neglect, including much recent research.

## Relationships

Gettingtheloveyouwant.com
Site for Imago Relationship Therapy, my favorite couples therapy approach.

Gottman.com
Site of John Gottman's Relationship Institute. Gottman is a marriage researcher with 40-plus years of data about what makes relationships successful and enduring.

Patlove.com
Site of Pat Love, relationship expert, therapist, and author of a number of useful books.

## Sexuality

AASECT.org
AASECT is the American Association of Sexuality Educators, Counselors, and Therapists, which certifies practitioners in the sexuality field. The site offers information and a directory for locating qualified sex therapists.

Dodsonandross.com
Site of Betty Dodson, pioneer sex researcher and therapist.

Plannedparenthood.org
Site of Planned Parenthood, a longstanding resource for reliable sex education.

## RECOMMENDED READING

Cassidy, Jude, and Shaver, Phillip, *Handbook of Attachment*. New York: Guilford, 2008.
Foley, Sallie, Kope, Sally, and Sugrue, Dennis, *Sex Matters for Women*. New York: Guilford, 2002.
Gottman, John, *Why Marriages Succeed or Fail*. New York: Fireside Books, 1994.
Hendrix, Harville, *Getting the Love You Want*. New York: Henry Holt and Co., 1988.
Herman, Judith, *Trauma and Recovery*. New York: Basic Books, 1992.
Levine, Peter, *Waking the Tiger*. Berkeley: North Atlantic Books, 1997.
Love, Pat, and Robinson, Jo, *Hot Monogamy*. New York: Penguin Books, 1994.
Love, Pat, and Stosny, Stephen, *How to Improve Your Marriage Without Talking About It*. New York: Random House, 2007.
Nelson, Tammy, *Getting the Sex You Want*. Beverly: Quiver Publishers, 2008.
Ogden, Pat, Minton, Kekuni, and Pain, Clare, *Trauma and the Body*. New York: Norton, 2006.

# NOTES

### CHAPTER ONE: IN THE BEGINNING: ATTACHMENT STYLES

Bowlby, John, *Attachment and Loss*. New York: Basic Books, 1969.

Cassidy, Jude, and Shaver, Phillip, *Handbook of Attachment*. New York: Guilford, 2008.

### CHAPTER THREE: DON'T GET ME WRONG! HD COMMUNICATION

Maya Kollman is an Imago Relationship therapist in Pennington, NJ. She gave me permission to use this quote. Maya said, "I don't remember where I got it but I did not make it up."

### CHAPTER SIX: IT'S THE END OF THE WORLD AS WE KNOW IT: A PRIMER ON TRAUMA

Rauch, S. L., van der Kolk, B., et al., "A Symptom Provocation Study of Posttraumatic Stress Disorder Using Positron Emission Tomography and Script Driven Imagery." *Archives of General Psychiatry* 57 (May 1996): 380–387.

### CHAPTER SEVEN: WAITING FOR THE SUN TO COME OUT: WAKING UP TO NEGLECT

Ed Hamlin is a psychologist at the Pisgah Center for the Advancement of Human Potential in Ashville, NC. He specializes in the effects of early trauma and neglect on the developing brain. He gave me permission to retell the story of his dog, Streak, told at the Boston Trauma Conference, June 2010.

Ainsworth, Mary, et al., *Patterns of Attachment: A Psychological Study of the Strange Situation*. New York: LEA, 1978.

## CHAPTER EIGHT: DO YOU WANNA DANCE? MORE ABOUT TRIGGERING AND ADAPTATION

Hesse, Erik, "The Adult Attachment Interview" in Cassidy, Jude, and Shaver, Phillip, eds., *Handbook of Attachment*. New York: Guilford, 2008.

## CHAPTER NINE: CYCLES OF ESCALATION: IT TAKES TWO TO TANGLE

Buzsaki, Gyorgy, *Rhythms of the Brain*. New York: Oxford University Press, 2006. p. 14.

## CHAPTER TWELVE: THIS THING CALLED LOVE: MYTHS AND FACTS ABOUT ADULT SEXUALITY

Dodson, Betty, *Self Loving*. DVD available through her website: dodsonandross.com.

Gottman, John and Gottman, Julie Schwartz, *And Baby Makes Three: The Six-Step Plan for Preserving Marital Intimacy and Rekindling Romance After Baby Arrives*. New York: Random House, 2007.

Kahr, Brett, *Who's Been Sleeping in Your Head: The Secret World of Sexual Fantasies*. New York: Basic Books, 2007

Kerner, Ian, *Love in the Time of Colic: The New Parents' Guide to Getting It on Again*. New York: Harper Collins, 2009.

Kleinplatz, Peggy, et al., "The Components of Optimal Sexuality: A Portrait of Great Sex." *Canadian Journal of Human Sexuality* 18 (1–2, 2009): 1–13.

Love, Pat, and Robinson, Jo, *Hot Monogamy*. New York: Penguin Books, 1994.

## CHAPTER SIXTEEN: THE WAY IT IS: ASSESSMENT

Fosha, Diana, *The Transforming Power of Affect*. New York: Basic Books, 2000.

## CHAPTER SEVENTEEN: HUMAN TOUCH: BEING HERE NOW

Linda Perlin Alperstein, MSW, LCSW, is an associate clinical professor in the UCSF Department of Psychiatry and a sex therapist practicing in San Francisco. I am indebted to her for the practices The Ideal Time and Place and The Guided Body Tour.

## CHAPTER EIGHTEEN: WE'RE ON OUR WAY HOME: MORE ABOUT PRESENCE AND SOME PRACTICE

Kleinplatz, Peggy, et al., "The Components of Optimal Sexuality: A Portrait of Great Sex." *Canadian Journal of Human Sexuality* 18 (1–2, 2009): 1–13.

David Yarian is a clinical psychologist and certified sex therapist in Nashville, TN. I am indebted to him for the Tantric Gazing and Heart Flow practices.

## CHAPTER NINETEEN: STARTING OVER: PRACTICE AND MORE PRACTICE

Allende, Isabel, *The Sum of Our Days: A Memoir*. New York: Harper Collins, 2008.

Carol Ellison is a psychologist, author and AASECT Certified Sex Therapist. Personal communication.

Linda Perlin Alperstein, MSW, LCSW, is an associate clinical professor in the UCSF Department of Psychiatry and a sex therapist practicing in San Francisco. I am indebted to her for the practices The Ideal Time and Place and the Guided Body Tours. Personal communication.

Masters, William, Johnson, Virginia, and Kolodny, Robert, *Human Sexuality*. New York: Little Brown and Co., 1982

## CHAPTER TWENTY: WHAT A LONG STRANGE TRIP IT'S BEEN: INTEGRATION, "RE-MEMBERING," AND RENEWAL

Levine, Peter, *Sexual Healing*. Audio Book. Louisville: Sounds True, Inc., 2003.

McCarthy, Barry, *Discovering Your Couple Sexual Style: Sharing Desire, Pleasure, and Satisfaction*. New York: Routledge, 2009.

# BIBLIOGRAPHY

Ainsworth, Mary, et al., *Patterns of Attachment: A Psychological Study of the Strange Situation*. New York: LEA, 1978.

Bowlby, John, *Attachment and Loss*. New York: Basic Books, 1969.

Buzsaki, Gyorgy, *Rhythms of the Brain*. New York: Oxford University Press, 2006.

Cassidy, Jude, and Shaver, Phillip, *Handbook of Attachment*. New York: Guilford, 2008.

Dodson, Betty, *Orgasms for Two: The Joy of Partnersex*. New York: Harmony Books, 2002.

Foley, Sallie, Kope, Sally, and Sugrue, Dennis, *Sex Matters for Women*. New York: Guilford, 2002.

Fosha, Diana, *The Transforming Power of Affect*. New York: Basic Books, 2000.

Gottman, John, *Why Marriages Succeed or Fail*. New York: Fireside Books, 1994.

Gottman, John, *The Seven Principles for Making Marriage Work: A Practical Guide from the Country's Foremost Relationship Expert*. New York: Random House, 1999.

Gottman, John, *The Relationship Cure: A 5 Step Guide to Strengthening Your Marriage, Family, and Friendships*. New York: Three Rivers Press, 2001.

Hendrix, Harville, *Getting the Love You Want*. New York: Henry Holt and Co., 1988.

Herman, Judith, *Trauma and Recovery*. New York: Basic Books, 1992.

Kahr, Brett, *Who's Been Sleeping in Your Head: The Secret World of Sexual Fantasies*. New York: Basic Books, 2007.

Kaschak, Ellen, and Tiefer, Lenore, eds., *A New View of Women's Sexual Problems*. Binghamton: Haworth Press, 2001.

Kleinplatz, Peggy, et al., "The Components of Optimal Sexuality: A Portrait of Great Sex." *Canadian Journal of Human Sexuality* 18 (1–2, 2009): 1–13.

Levine, Peter, *Waking the Tiger*. Berkeley: North Atlantic Books, 1997.

Levine, Peter, *Sexual Healing*. Audio Book. Louisville: Sounds True, Inc., 2003.

Love, Pat, and Robinson, Jo, *Hot Monogamy*. New York: Penguin Books. 1994.

Love, Pat, and Stosny, Stephen, *How to Improve Your Marriage Without Talking About It*. New York: Random House. 2007.

Masters, William, Johnson, Virginia, and Kolodny, Robert, *Human Sexuality*. New York: Little Brown and Co., 1982.

McCarthy, Barry, *Discovering Your Couple Sexual Style: Sharing Desire, Pleasure, and Satisfaction*. New York: Routledge, 2009.

Morin, Jack, *The Erotic Mind*. New York: Harper Collins, 1995.

Nelson, Tammy, *Getting the Sex You Want*. Beverly: Quiver Publishers, 2008.

Northrup, Christiane, *The Wisdom of Menopause*. New York: Bantam, 2001.

Ogden, Pat, Minton, Kekuni, and Pain, Clare, *Trauma and the Body*. New York: Norton, 2006.

Pert, Candace, *Molecules of Emotion*. New York: Scribner, 1997.

Rauch, S. L., van der Kolk, B., et al., "A Symptom Provocation Study of Posttraumatic Stress Disorder Using Positron Emission Tomography and Script Driven Imagery." *Archives of General Psychiatry* 57 (May 1996): 380–387.

Scaer, Robert, *The Body Bears the Burden*. Binghamton: Haworth Press, 2001.

Schore, Alan, *Affect Regulation and the Origin of the Self: The Neurobiology of Emotional Development*. Hillsdale: Lawrence Erlbaum Associates, 1994.

Siegel, Daniel, *The Developing Mind*. New York: Guilford, 1999.

Van der Kolk, Bessel, MacFarlane, Alexander, and Weiseth, Lars, *Traumatic Stress: The Effects of Overwhelming Experience on Mind, Body and Society*. New York: Guilford, 1996.

# INDEX

## About the Author

RUTH COHN is Marriage and Family Therapist and AASECT Certified Sex Therapist living in San Francisco. She has specialized in working with trauma survivors and their intimate partners and families since 1987. In 1997 she developed a special interest in working with couples. Largely from her own marriage, she discovered that the intimate partnership takes people to depths in themselves beyond those they can get to any other way. It can also be a vehicle for perhaps the most profound healing imaginable. Inspired, she began to evolve this theory and practice of working with couples who have histories of trauma and neglect.

Ruth is trained in Harville Hendrix's Imago Relationship Therapy, which is an important component of her work. Because trauma is so much an experience of the nervous system and the entire body, she became an impassioned student of brain science, the body psychotherapies, and neurofeedback, which also strongly influence her thinking and practice. She loves working with couples and sustains great hope and optimism about the potential for healing both intimacy and sexuality.

## About the Series Editor

JUDY KURIANSKY, PhD, is an internationally known licensed clinical psychologist. She is also on the adjunct faculty in the Department of Clinical Psychology at Columbia University Teachers College and in the Department of Psychiatry at Columbia University College of Physicians and Surgeons. At the United Nations, she is a nongovernmental organization representative for the International Association of Applied Psychology and for the World Council for Psychotherapy, and is on the Executive Committee of the Committee of Mental Health. She is also a visiting professor at the Peking University Health Sciences Center, a Fellow of the American Psychological Association, a cofounder of the APA Media Psychology Division, and a member of the board of the Peace Division and of U.S. Doctors for Africa. A certified sex therapist by the American Association of Sex Educators and Counselors, she is a pioneer in the field of sexuality, setting standards, writing innumerable books about the subject, giving advice in many formats and speaking at conferences worldwide. An award-winning journalist, she hosted the popular LovePhones syndicated call-in radio show for years as well as the TV show "Money and Emotions" on CNBC-TV, was a feature reporter for WCBS-TV and WABC-TV, and now regularly comments on news and current events for television worldwide as well as for print media, including as a columnist for Bottom Line Women's Health among other magazines, newspapers and online forums. As a humanitarian, her Stand Up for Peace Project and band does symposia and concerts worldwide. Her wide-ranging expertise from interpersonal to international relations is evident in her books, with titles ranging from *The Complete Idiot's Guide to a Healthy Relationship, Generation Sex,* and *Sexuality Education: Past, Present and Future* to *Beyond Bullets and Bombs: Grassroots Peacebuilding between Israelis and Palestinians.* Her Web site is www.DrJudy.com.